Eighteenth-Century Painting

Compass History of Art

Edited by André Held and D. W. Bloemena

The complete series includes:

Eighteenth-Century Painting

Vassily Photiades

THE VIKING PRESS
New York

A COMPASS BOOKS original edition

Published in 1964 by The Viking Press, Inc.

625 Madison Avenue, New York 10022, N.Y.

Library of Congress catalog card number: 63–15220

Printed in Holland

Contents

On doit toujours s'excuser de parler peinture
PAUL VALÉRY

Eighteenth-Century Painting

Introduction

Apart from five great artists, two of them belonging to the French School, European painting of the eighteenth century is distinctly less rich than that of the centuries before and after it. This is perhaps not the general view, but it is at least certain that the age of elegance suffers from what might be called a halo of excessive seductiveness. It is undoubtedly in this too systematically pursued seductiveness, this too consciously sought and deliberate *elegance*, that its relative weakness lies. But this century has given us five admirable painters who to a large extent redeem its prevailing mediocrity. They do in fact tend to make us forget the Mannerism of a period of European painting which at least produced an impressive number of minor painters, a harvest of over-skilful and often charming – perhaps too charming – executants.

If one tries to take a bird's eye view as it were of the history of painting in time and space, it is easy to see it as a sort of graph, like a temperature chart, with its peaks and troughs. To try to discover the laws governing this rise and fall would be a utopian project, and art historians who attempt to make sense of these fluctuations give us unconvincing reasons for them. There are occasional exceptions, however; we come across periods of rich flowering or of decadence in the history of the plastic arts which seem to have a more rational basis. Thus the relative weakness of eighteenth-century painting seems to be the result of a decline into facile conventionality, a reaction towards laxity after the severe and lofty disciplines prevalent during the reign of Louis XIV.

If we compare an armchair or a chest of drawers of Louis XIV's reign with similar objects from the reign of his successor, Louis the Well-Beloved, the contrast is significant if somewhat over-simplified. But, though today we may happen to prefer – and it is merely a question of fashion

– the sinuous elegance of a Louis XV chest of drawers or an armchair in which one of his favourites reclined, to the more monumental, richer and severer solidity of the same articles of furniture from Louis XIV's reign, it is not the same with painting. We certainly do not hesitate to relegate a painter who was for some time Diderot's god – Greuze, together with his moralizing confections – to the tenth category, and prefer to him one of the greatest French painters of the seventeenth century – Poussin.

Does the same hold good for Italy? The contrast is possibly greater here, because we have to compare the masters of the sixteenth century, some of whom overlap into the seventeenth, with a very short list of artists – there are three in fact – all provided by Venice, and Venice alone. In the century we are considering, can Tiepolo, for instance, who remains a dazzlingly accomplished decorator, be compared to the distinguished painters who preceded him and who made Italian painting – quite apart from its incomparable sculpture – the richest and most splendid school that has ever existed in the history of the plastic arts? We must remember, too, that what has been justly described as the 'Italian miracle' lasted for five centuries without a pause – in fact, that painting was invented in Italy.

And what must be said of English painters during the century under discussion, if we are to have the courage of our convictions? Although the case is somewhat similar to that of France, we must remember that the latter country has provided two masters belonging unquestionably to the first rank – Watteau and Chardin – and that it is far otherwise with England. It is interesting to notice that though England bears the palm for European poetry, and her output of novelists is admirable, she is not a country favourable to the blossoming of the plastic arts, with three apparently accidental exceptions – Constable, Bonington and Turner, all really belonging to the nineteenth century. To return to our period, English painting clearly manifests the same weaknesses as French, with two very important differences: that the insipidity typical of the eighteenth century is more dangerously apparent, and that it is almost entirely represented by portrait painters, although at least two of these are of some importance.

There remains Spain, where a single remarkable genius puts all his contemporary compatriots in the shade. I refer, of course, to Goya. But it must be emphasized that he hardly represents his epoch. His is an exceptional case, in complete contrast with the spirit of his century. In fact he seems to be apart from it, as if outside of time, and his own time in particular, and advancing towards the future.

To sum up: eighteenth-century painting is, with a few superb exceptions, the least rich and the least original in the history of the plastic arts, and its representatives are for the most part relatively inferior. Some will see in this the end of an epoch whose fast approaching collapse these paintings were proclaiming; others will lay the blame on the lassitude, exhaustion and senescence of a decadent society; of a society – and this was true for all Europe – that was concentrated on pleasure alone, drifting along in the line of least resistance, as happens in every country on the verge of ruin. It may be that this is applicable only to schools which pay tribute to a state-controlled art or a constricted social order, and it seems to be notably false whenever the creative impulse develops and blossoms in a period of individualism.

An instance of this is to be found in France during the nineteenth century. At the same time that the school of the Académie des Beaux Arts was reflecting in no uncertain manner the mediocrity of official and bourgeois art, masterly but very different work was being produced in obscurity by independent painters, in revolt against all established art and aesthetics, and against a society that was ill-provided with patrons or art-lovers having sufficient authority and clearsightedness to single out and defend those who were to found a new and glorious school (beginning with Delacroix and his dramatic victories). That was exactly what happened to the precursors of Impressionism. Let me try to illustrate my point by finding non-conformists in other periods in the history of painting. Uccello was not despised or scorned for revolutionizing painting by perspective; van Eyck was not penalized for introducing the new technique of oil-painting to Europe; and no one was scandalized when Giorgione and Titian established the primacy of colour.

Then why was Manet discredited for exhibiting his *Olympia*, so reminiscent of Velázquez and even more of Goya? It was because Florence and Venice were thronged with 'Medicis' – connoisseurs and rich patrons – whereas in nineteenth-century France it was left to Baudelaire to show judgment in opposition to the whole of Paris, and go almost alone to the defence of his idol Delacroix, and also of Courbet and Manet.

People jeer too often and too stupidly nowadays at Taine's famous obsession with the environment, which probably has more truth in it than they suppose. They are readier to lend a strangely attentive ear to the very indifferent art criticisms of that excellent poet Apollinaire. Let us admit, as M. François Fosca has had the courage to do, that he certainly did not excel as a writer about art. Yet his stumbling, foolish, childish utterances are echoed by our wretched art critics, who vie with one another in treating the remarks of a puerile mystificator as Gospel truth. But we must return to the 'environment'. It is mainly to environmental conditions that I, for my part, attribute the relative, but indubitable weakness of painting in the century we are studying. There is no need to overstress the point; we must not forget the unbelievable lack of understanding that Poussin met with from high society and the Court when he was painting his masterpieces.

It is on the whole wiser not to try too hard to find a rational explanation for the blossoming of art in one period and its decline in another. But it is very tempting to formulate cautious hypotheses. Platitudes sometimes contain important truths: and these are always the hardest to accept.

Watteau *(figs. 1–13)*

It can be said of Watteau not only that (Chardin apart) he dominates his century, but also that from every point of view he occupies an important position in the history of painting. By this I mean that he has devised a world of his own – a kingdom that one is tempted to call Shakespearian when remembering the lyrical fairyland created by the great English poet. This word *poet* comes inevitably to mind whenever one tries to define Watteau's work as a painter. I shall try to explain why; but before beginning such an analysis I must attempt another, although it is strictly speaking chimerical. I mean the insoluble problem of discovering the reasons which make one say of a painting that it contains and communicates a poetic quality as well as colour and form.

The title of poet is too readily given nowadays to those who work with palette and brush, and it must be admitted that it is often misapplied. Our age is prodigal of epithets, and the adjective 'poetic' is distributed so generously that it has largerly lost its meaning. We must be grateful to the very few artists who give it back its true significance. But to begin with let us try and get a clearer idea of what is understood by the word 'poetry' when applied to painting. Of all vocabularies that of the aesthetician is the most imprecise and it has degenerated into mere jargon today; confusion and inexactitudes are so numerous, and hold such easy sway, that it sometimes seems as if it were made up of nothing else.

I must admit that I believe this mysterious symbiosis of form, coloured pigments and poetry is as completely impenetrable as the famous concept of 'pure poetry', all attempts to give a valid definition of which have failed, even when the interpreters were such celebrated initiates as Gide, Valéry or the Abbé Brémond. Despite their magnifying-glasses and their special clairvoyance, pure poetry will preserve its wonderful secret for ever, so I believe. But I must try to explain what is meant when we say that a painter is also a poet. In point of fact it is rather easier to say why he is not; why some great artist has never been a poet, as is the case with such eminent painters as Veronese or Manet. There are geniuses who figure in the history of art and are not poets, just as there are less important artists who possess this rare and incomprehensible quality. It is obvious that Titian, Botticelli, Corot, Brueghel and Watteau, to mention no others, carried the lyre in addition to being marvellous painters. They did so in different manners, a fact which complicates the problem; for example Turner, whose poetry is concerned with visions of sky and light, certainly has nothing in common with Brueghel, whose Muse has made him a story-teller, a narrator from whose imagery rises the echoing music of an inspired fabulist. Finally, to make it harder still to find the way out of the maze, it must be said that painter-poets only reach this particular kingdom by way of reality, or what we usually describe as such. For, in this strange world of painting, poetry flies away as soon as one tries to catch it, but settles tamely to rest with the painter who is not giving it a thought.

So it is to this astonishingly small family of lyric painters that Watteau belongs. This quality is so apparent in him that it is perceived even by the outsider, the uninitiated, to whom the secrets of painting are unknown territory. But before going deeper into the poetic character of his work, let us first discuss its purely pictorial qualities.

His colour range is a very personal one. Silver greys, clear or subdued blues, violets (dull in spite of their brilliance) and a weak autumnal yellow merging into dull gold, meet, come to terms or are skilfully made to conflict, setting in motion shivers of light and vibrant reflections. But if this enumeration should call to mind a lifeless palette, it is nothing of the kind. Watteau's tonality is always full of depth and mysterious luminosity; it has something in common with the deep, velvet register of a cello – if the simile may be allowed. The dress of a young woman with her back to us in *Gersaint's Sign Board* may serve as an example; it is of a pinkish lilac so subtle and delicate that it seems to be secretly gliding towards white.

There is no doubt that this Frenchman from the north was endowed with the gift of creating pictorial texture, that is to say that oily texture, rich in thick, solid pigments, that creamy enamel which is the property of what has been called pure painting. The secret was unknown to Florence, but the Venetian School possessed it from the first, and it was brought to perfection by painters such as Giambono, Guariento and Titian. It seemed to come naturally to Watteau, and we must not forget that his native town of Valenciennes was only a few yards from Flanders, a region whose chief artists, van Eyck, Memling, Rembrandt, Hals and Vermeer, were all gifted in this way, like the Dutch School.

It has often been remarked that most of Watteau's subjects come from the Italian theatre, which had a great success under Louis XV, and must often have been seen by the painter from his earliest youth. But what does it matter what subjects Watteau chose? Whether he paints historical sub-jects, flowers, portraits or landscapes, the important thing is what the artist makes of them, the style he imposes on them and the way in which he transforms them. So that we shall not lay any great stress on Watteau's subjects, nor follow the definitions of those numerous art critics who declare that the themes which inspired our artist came from the scenery and stage upon which the *Commedia dell'Arte* mounted the traditional characters of the Bergamask. This view probably originated with Jules de Goncourt, who wrote extremely well about eighteenth-century painting, although this did not prevent him showing partiality for minor painters hardly deserving the laurels he bestowed on them. The persistence of this critical attitude is strange in view of the fact that figures from the Bergamask certainly do not dominate Watteau's works, even if a few contain references to them. For instance, the landscapes which serve as background to them and with which they are so wonderfully integrated, are inspired by nature alone and never represent cut-out scenery, or cardboard trees pushed on to the stage. Perhaps his costumes gave rise to the legend, for his figures are often dressed in the Italian style. But at least three-quarters of Watteau's work has no reference to the theatre. This is too easily demonstrated for it to be necessary to prove it here. And when our painter-poet does represent scenes from the French theatre, they are never illuminated by footlights; he prefers natural daylight instead of special stage lighting such as is seen in Degas's ballets, and he represents its effects like the great landscape-painter he is. It is a pleasure to remember a phrase of Elie Faure's to the effect that the setting sun which glows on Claude Lorrain's canvases is pure Watteau! Renoir understood this well when he praised the superb landscape in which skilfully grouped figures move and converse in *La Fête d'Amour* in the Dresden Museum. And here, without realizing it, we have arrived at one of Watteau's greatest gifts, that of combining his human figures with the landscape surrounding them in a marvellously homogeneous unity. To possess this gift to such a perfect degree is much rarer than might be supposed; hardly any but the great Venetians were capable of conceiving and carrying out such a harmonious fusion of figures, trees, the horizon and the sky itself. Delacroix is, of course, the last great European painter to have this talent, and we think also of Manet's *Déjeuner sur l'Herbe*, which is perhaps the most recent and finest example – but, to return to our problem, we must add that this superb canvas is quite without 'poetry' of any sort.

Let us now come to grips with our subject and try to discover why this poetry which was lacking in Manet and most other painters, even painters of genius, is to be found in Watteau's canvases. It is tempting to say that the chief reason for their profound, musical and sometimes heart-rending melancholy is that this artist's work is concerned with the image of happiness. And what is more fragile, elusive and transient? But that is not all. To this ephemeral quality is added an atmosphere emphasizing everything connected with disappearance, the fall of night, twilight. Almost all Watteau's skies are in fact twilit, bathed in that evening light which affects all human beings with the same faint sadness. We are discreetly informed that we are witnessing the close of day, and the end of what is essentially perishable – love. Love takes on a very special significance here. I am not thinking of the love of the *Fêtes Galantes*, where 'Pleasure reigns supreme' as Watteau's commentators say; this subject was treated by his followers Fragonard and Boucher, with whom I believe he has nothing in common*. Let us think for a moment of the numerous couples of citizens of Valenciennes, and surprise them in the splendid landscapes they inhabit.

Their exquisitely reserved gestures full of courtesy and tenderness, their soft embraces, their clasped hands, are all signs that they are lovers, but above all they are expressions of *sentiment* – a sentiment in which sensual pleasure is represented only by a phantom floating around them like a vague promise, a hardly conscious anticipation, whose secret presence is, as it were, in the background.

These people whisper and murmur together, they enjoy a community of sensibilities and sentiment, a mutual understanding all the more precious because it is threatened by the passing of time, ever walking at their side. As a final touch the surrounding trees are mostly russet-coloured, as if they too had been affected by the end of the season, by autumn – symbol of repeated farewells; they are tinged a faded gold by the transient light of the setting sun. If I am to choose one profoundly characteristic picture by Watteau, a picture bathed in that magic atmosphere typical of his melancholy sorcery, perhaps it should be the *Figures in a Park* (fig. 7) in the Louvre. The film of harmony spread over this canvas is even more concentrated than usual, and combines with the velvet silence it gives off. The basic realism with which the scene is observed has given us a superb landscape, with great trees spreading their branches against a sky which softly proclaims the close of day and is repeated in the calm waters of a pond. Although there are a dozen figures in the foreground, the solitude of the place is more potent than their presence, and the clear, delicate light which shines on them outlines their postures and forms with a complicated luminous filigree. The folds of their clothes, the subtle modelling of their necks, bosoms, hands and coiffures are emphasized with extraordinary economy and exemplary simplicity. A couple standing on the left of this perfect composition seem to have come to a tender understanding. On the right, a group of five figures make up an arabesque of dull tones, while one of them appears to be interpreting the musical serenity of the moment on a shadowy flute in the gloaming. And in the centre of this masterpiece stands a little girl with her back to us, like an attentive fairy, joining us in motionless contemplation of the enchanted moment fixed by the magician Watteau upon the dial of the fleeting hours.

* *The False Step* (fig. 10) in the Louvre (exactly copied in the *Fête d'Amour* of the Dresden Museum) is the single exception reproduced in this book. But how discreet a page it is beside the works of Watteau's followers, many of which are frankly licentious.

The author of these lines writes as a painter, and begs the reader not to see anything literary in his attempt at an analysis of *poetry* which is after all produced only by means of form and colour. Colour and form clearly play an important part in this unconscious lyricism, and both are transmuted by the painter's personal vision of nature – of the trees, for instance, whose spreading shapes are poised between the convincing naturalism of a marvellously accurate observer and some indefinable dream that Watteau carried within him. It is an intoxicating union of precision and vagueness, of vision and observation, perfectly blended in a skilful amalgam which allows one a glimpse of the secret composition of the philtre. Even if the first thing the initiate admires is the subtle tonality of a palette reminiscent of the musical harmony of Giorgione or Titian – I am thinking of the *Concert Champêtre* in the Louvre which I believe to be undoubtedly by the latter – he cannot be oblivious of the way in which Watteau's colours and harmonies add their own lyricism to the other poetic qualities of the inspired musician that he is. To complete this portrait of work that is impregnated with false vagueness and illusory precision, with something hazy, dreamlike and unreal, let me say that it is built on a skeleton of exemplary solidity – that of good drawing, of impeccable, individual and masterly draughtsmanship, full of nervous strength. Together with his skill as a colourist, it has acted as a springboard to project Watteau in triumph towards the heights of poetry and dreams. We are concerned with an exceptional case in the history of painting, and in spite of all our analysis and explanation he preserves his secret intact. It is a secret that Watteau doubtless shares with such admirable masters as Titian, whose Venuses make audible the same silence vibrating with dreams, a secret uniting three deities rarely found together. Here, in these incomparable works, we find them closely intertwined. Their names are Form, Colour, and Watteau's own ineffable and original Poetry.

Chardin *(figs. 14–25)*

Only a painter can explain exactly why Chardin is a great painter. But it is the fashion for writers about art to repeat the clichés brought to his defence. These clichés are to some extent valid but they do not go far to explain how it is that all creators of still-lifes of every period are inferior to Chardin. Of course, he combines objects, fruit, fish, game, and all the other traditional elements of a still-life with austerely classical perfection. This is a valid statement, just as it is valid to point to the subtlety of his compositions and colour harmonies. But the rigorous skill used in their construction, the fact that the number, volume and choice of objects are utilized to make an admirably balanced whole, does not explain the exquisite delicacy of his palette or the perfection of his modelling. This painter's secret must be looked for elsewhere. It is to be found in his *values*. It is always difficult to explain this term to laymen, yet a clear definition makes it easily comprehensible by anyone, and reveals its extreme simplicity. These famous values consist in the graduated scale uniting white and black, or light and dark.

There is no great difficulty in imagining the infinite gradations of this scale going from black to dark grey, and thence to pale grey and white. But it must be remembered that a similar scale exists for every colour – for blue, for instance, leading from the deepest cobalt to white with a suspicion of blue in it. It is because of these values, miraculously perceived by a particularly sensitive eye that Chardin stands upon one of the pinnacles of what we have called pure painting. Herein lies his power, his striking originality, the main characteristic of his personality as a painter. Is his case unique? Certainly not; he has his equals, but they are very few. One could name one or two among them with a retina capable of discerning and registering these minute nuances, and therefore able to model the thousand forms of visible reality, and – more important still – to transform them in the process. Among those blessed with this rare gift, the Dutch painter Vermeer stands in the first rank, along with Corot. Cézanne devoted himself with passion and industry to this most difficult of aims: to model a given form – or 'modulate' it, as he liked to say – by precision of values alone. His success was remarkable, particularly with still-lifes and portraits, and we must not forget that by returning to the same subject a hundred times he finally succeeded in painting apples, for example, so that innumerable superimposed layers of paint created a sort of roughcast, an eloquent and living image of the battle he had been waging. If he had not the facility to carry out his projects within a reasonable space of time he at least had the faculty of exact vision. And Corot, prince of landscape-painters and an admirable figure-painter, achieved a subtlety comparable with Cézanne's by painting with a feather, hardly covering the canvas, and yet producing a masterpiece of density, solidity and freshness, where the most delicate colour-values have been reached at a single stroke as it were, to judge by the thinness of the paint. I am thinking of the *Bridge at Narni*, and of the study of the same subject, with its miraculous chromatic richness. This landscape is not the harbinger of Impressionism, it already belongs to that as yet non-existent school! From this comparison we may gather that Cézanne *toils* and Corot *sings*.

As for Chardin's technique, it would seem that, without having anything in common with Cézanne's constantly renewed endeavours, his persistence, his struggles, 'Chardin's slowness' was mentioned by his contemporaries, a slowness of another order from Cézanne's laboriousness. His is the work of an enameller, of a craftsman who loves his craft and polishes his surface, spreading smooth, even layers of paint without being in any hurry to give the final touch to his canvas. All that counts for him is perfect workmanship, whether in composition, form or (above all) colour-values, not to mention his admirable harmonies, where there is no trace of hesitation, where nothing is left to chance. Here everything is weighed, deliberately decided upon and – in a word – conscious. An anecdote repeated by M. François Fosca is interesting, whether it be true or false: it seems that one of Chardin's fellow-painters was telling him how much easier it was to paint cabbages than the human figure. According to the story, this chance remark was responsible for the fact that our still-life painter became adept at painting other subjects, such as scenes from his own home life in the Dutch manner. These scenes have all the marvellous qualities of his still-lifes while adding others to them, such as extreme simplicity, and a naturalness that is rare in a period where all is affectation and conventional grace, with the exception, of course of the incomparable Watteau. Thus scenes such as *The Cateress* (fig. 14) or *The Teacher*, *The Boy with the Spinning-Top* (fig. 16), or *The Little Girl with the Shuttlecock* (fig. 22) show us Chardin's gifts applied to the human figure. We find in them the same marvellously enamelled surface, the same design and composition, and a colour harmony of a very unusual resonance. They are splendid masterpieces, comparable to those of Vermeer, or even – I will be bold enough to say – surpassing the sometimes rather cold, frozen works of the great Dutchman by their perfect warmth and freedom. We can see Chardin and Watteau, then, as the highest peaks of the eighteenth century. If the latter dominates his age by reason of all the rare gifts we have mentioned, the former does so also, while still belonging (in spite of appearances) to the French eighteenth century, an age of rationalism and austerity, the age of Descartes, an age which is mirrored to perfection in Chardin's still-lifes, conceived and executed like diagrams or theorems. This does not prevent the carpenter's son from displaying marvellous sensuality of colour, the chief source of his greatness. Moreover, like the modest craftsman he was, in splendid isolation among the salons and brilliant wits in which his epoch abounded, he directed his attention towards the silence of inanimate things, towards everyday reality, towards that intimate family life whose secret sweetness he did not even try to glorify, because he felt it to be the very image of happiness, as indeed it is. He left it to the superficial painters of his day to provide a surrogate, a phantom, a mime; for his individual sensuality is a painter's sensuality, such that everything, from a plum to a jar of milk, is transformed by his personal vision into something which makes our mouths water, something which clamours for the long slow caress of our gaze. It is amusing to hear art critics insist on the extreme *humbleness* of the objects our artist chooses to portray. They even go so far as to say that Chardin was expressing his political convictions in this manner and revealing his 'proletarian' tendencies! This is absurd, and typical also of recent developments in art criticism. For my part, I have searched for signs of political commitment in vain! Chardin is doing much as Oudry did when he painted household articles, and one may admire in his still-lifes valuable flagons, glasses delicately traced with gold, or precious china appropriate to a prosperous bourgeois household. Delacroix lovingly painted a humble stove, and Chardin's cauldrons seem to be made of eighteen carat gold . . .

I should like to end these few pages on Chardin by trying to describe his marvellous palette. I know that words are weak and hazardous instruments for such a transmutation; the plastic arts, like music, have their own language, and it is futile to try to translate it into words. Sometimes one is led to make the attempt (by its very nature illusory) out of love and admiration for a particular work, and the temptation to transmit this love and admiration as exactly as possible is so great that even a painter, who knows the vanity and impossibility of translation, will murmur something as he stands before the passionately loved canvas, in an effort to underline the qualities and character of a palette in words. He is really doing it for his own sake, as one takes notes of a work of art in order to remember it better, to preserve one's own memory of it.

We are at this moment standing in front of a still-life called *Dessert* (fig. 19), in the Louvre. There are very few objects on the canvas, but it is a harmonious masterpiece, and the light that bathes it is the light of silence. In the centre of the composition a splendid loaf reigns supreme, and above its broad crust, appetizingly browned in the oven, is a little spray of flowers, like a triumphant crown. The loaf displays its superb texture, diversified by cookery into a symphony of brown and white. In the foreground are a couple of small but delicious-looking peaches, united by their shadow, while on the extreme left a sugar-bowl strikes a singing note of that admirable white invented by Chardin, which is to be found in his enamel pots, his china objects and his clothes – from the warm white of *The Teacher* to the bluish tinge of the youthful cap of *The Little Girl with the Shuttlecock* (fig. 22) with its smooth and vibrant paint. I know no colours so seductive as Chardin's whites, except perhaps Manet's sumptuous blacks. But to return to our still-life. This time, look to the right of this regal loaf. There are three dry biscuits – but nothing in Chardin is dry – three cherries and a beautiful flask of wine the colour of the setting sun. The shining gold of the stopper is related to that of the loaf, echoes the tawny skins of the fruit, the clearer gold of the biscuits and the paler tinge of the sugar-bowl – a secret and supremely subtle harmony, of incomparable delicacy, with its half tones and its variegated shadows. The Dutch painters of still-life merely seem charming decorators when we think of this loaf (I have taken it as an example, but it is typical Chardin), this delicate flask, this china sugar-bowl; they were truly built to traverse the eternal river of time 'as a stone traverses water'.

The French School

I must warn my reader that I shall not obey a fixed chronological order in the survey I have undertaken, though this will not prevent my under-lining relationships, noting influences, making comparisons, and empha-sizing contrasts between the artists discussed. I have chosen rather to outline the plastic qualities and the original contributions made by certain painters – few in number – the dominant figures among whom are Watteau and Chardin, to whom the two preceding sections were devoted. But it is clear that as we stroll through the French eighteenth century in the follow-ing pages some of the artists of the second rank will try to evade our intended impartiality and gain a better place for themselves – Fragonard for instance. Shall I resist him and replace his name by that of some other painter personally more sympathetic to me? I think not; more especially as I shall still have space to emphasize the merits and qualities of some less famous painters, whose talents, though not so obvious or so spec-tacular, perhaps conceal more accomplishments beneath their apparent modesty.

Fragonard (figs. 26–34)

How difficult it is to be quite fair to Fragonard! The fanatical admiration some have for his work is a constant source of genuine astonishment to me. One must of course allow the 'fiery Frago' his vitality and spirit, recognize his passion for light, the insistence on the theme of pleasure revealed in his *Fêtes Galantes*, and the sincerity and frankness with which the sensuality of his subjects is emphasized. We have come a long way from Boucher and his artificiality. His somewhat coarse and questionable taste eagerly pursues the triumphs of carnal satisfaction. But he does so by means of too deliberate strategy, and the effect is spoilt by his clumsy contriving.

One must at least allow that Fragonard was driven by an authentic demon, animating all his work: the demon of virtuosity. He fell a victim to it in the end. This virtuosity is in the last resort his most striking charac-teristic and has prevented him becoming what he should have been: a major artist. It is only necessary to compare him briefly with Watteau for the weakness arising from this uncontrollable facility to leap to the eye. Never once does he try to dominate it, to force it to a slower pace, direct it, rein it in and make himself its master. In fact, he puts his horse into a gallop without holding the reins, and his unquestionable talent is seriously compromised by his passive acceptance of this necessarily superficial *brio*, whose servant he is. Verlaine gives a piece of advice in his *Art of Poetry* which might have been his saving: 'Take eloquence by the neck and strangle it', says the poet. But Fragonard is intoxicated by his own gifts as an improviser. As soon as he has set light to his firework set-piece he becomes a dazzled spectator. He is happy and active, enchanted by his own rapid manual dexterity. He tries everything and is delighted and astonished when he always succeeds. Erotic, historical or rustic subjects, scenes in the home or out of doors, portraits, landscapes – all were undertaken, attempted, skimmed over by this supremely gifted man, with such dexterity that he had no need to ponder for a moment over his sources of inspiration, or go more deeply into what he found attractive and charming. In a word, his only enemy was his excess of talent.

Am I being unjust? In appearance only, for I have arrived at my judgment by way of comparisons. This has led to my air of severity. But rather than be led to make a pale and timid classification, giving everyone more than his due, it is surely better to assess failings and virtues as clearly and boldly as possible. So in spite of appearances, it is fairer to Fragonard to show on the one hand how inferior he essentially is to a universal genius like Watteau, and on the other how he outclasses the charming trivialities of a painter like Boucher, over-valued though these were by a lax and superficial society. There are among Boucher's works some excellent portraits all the same and, when he abandoned his usual servility and stopped pandering to the tastes of the period, he produced some canvases revealing real painting. However, there is nothing in common between him and his pupil, the dazzling Fragonard.

Let us narrow the field a little by choosing one of the latter's drawings at random. Let us look at one of his beautiful landscapes in sanguine, where a few trees grouped in a masterly manner play the most important part. Confronted by nature, and absorbed in his model, it seems as if Fragonard forgets himself in the task of faithfully representing and analysing what lies before his eyes. One is full of admiration for the acuteness and penetration of his sensibility, the love and sincerity displayed by this artist when there is no question of showing off. 'I condemn the painter who shows off', wrote Delacroix in his Journal. Here, it is plain, Fragonard is working for his own satisfaction. The simply outlined masses of foliage, where light wars with shadow against the sky, quiver with life and truth. A spontaneous synthesis has eliminated details, distributed shadows, made the sun vibrate on the rich clumps of vegetation. He translates them with a hand which knows how to wait and then how to carry out the orders of a vigorous eye, passionately submitted to what it sees and what it wants to borrow from life. It is the same story when he sets out a composition on his page with pen and wash, grouping his figures, arranging a scene, as for instance in his *Dreamer,* who rests on her folded arms in front of her mirror, while two silent witnesses refrain from disturbing her light sleep. It is now that we realize what sort of a painter Fragonard could have been: a very great artist, deserving the name of master.

Boucher (figs. 49–54)

François Boucher never had a similar chance. If his pupil dissipated his gifts by trying to dazzle himself – with a not unsympathetic ingenuousness – Boucher himself was a calculating merchant of quack medicines, or concocter of aphrodisiacs, whose speculative shrewdness cannot long escape the observant eye. Of course he was the victim of his age; he was dedicated to fashion alone, and licentiousness was its chief characteristic. But there is no doubt at all that he overstepped the limits, and heaped all the gifts he possessed at the foot of an altar which was not dedicated to pleasure, as it appeared to be. 'For there is no nobler and more charming game than that of carnal pleasure', wrote Henri de Régnier in a series of amorous sketches in the style of the eighteenth century, and one only needs to repeat these words to unmask the systematic lie perpetrated by François Boucher, painter to the King and later exclusively attached to the service of the Marquise de Pompadour. His 'voluptuous' work, carried out 'in cold blood' is full of every artifice. Never has more deceptive homage been done to Venus. The offering has been paid in forged currency. Trickery reigns supreme, and it is with gloomy irritation that we see this painter, who in his day was a good colourist and a skilful draughtsman, decide to dedicate his work to old age and its belated cravings.

He made use of everything tending to this end. Ingeniously crumpled sheets, deranged pillows and unmade or half-open beds languidly support buttocks and torsos, dimpled arms and thighs bursting with plumpness, in scenes of detailed debauchery. This bedroom-sized universe, made up of curves and protuberances, of calculated abandon and often coarse provocation spiced with false candour, is further lavishly tricked out with ribbons, mirrors and revealing flounces, with fluttering cupids holding paper arrows and cardboard quivers. What we have here is an ambush; a snare, fit to catch only the palest phantom of sensual delight. Physical love, or Pandemos, the earthly Aphrodite of Greek mythology, can be impressive in a very different way; one only has to think of Rembrandt's licentious works to be aware that this is a pale simulacrum. In François Boucher's work, pleasure has the air of a masquerade.

Lancret (figs. 35–42)

Lancret's case is very different; one observes fewer meretricious qualities in him. From a temporary friendship with Watteau, who thought his early work promising, the pupil remained faithful to the style and themes of his master, even to the great draughtsman's calligraphy. Of course, Lancret was never more than Watteau's disciple, but he sincerely accepted the important lesson the master taught. Yet there is no denying that there is something stiff and rather laboured about his paintings, though he lacked neither genuine sensibility – shown even more in his drawings – nor a real eye for colour. His attractive canvases won him considerable success and, after the death of Gillot and Watteau, he became the fashion and had more work than he could do; this must have filled him with delight, for he was a hard worker ardently devoted to his profession, and somewhat addicted to *Fêtes Galantes*, though he deserves credit for their decorum in comparison to Boucher's servile artifices.

We cannot therefore refuse our sympathy to Watteau's admirer who, humble reflection though he was, also possessed a certain subtlety and an admirable dissatisfaction with himself and his work. This speaks volumes for his character as an honest artist who seems to have inherited a little of Watteau's nervous vitality, especially in the domain of draughtsmanship.

But are we not faced with a sort of twilight after the disappearance of the painter of *The Embarkment for Cythera*? The number of artists who preceded and followed Watteau is however impressive, and I must at least mention some names worthy of this position. Moreover most of them show such close relationship with one another – imposed, it is true, by the demands of their school and by a society that loved pleasure and epidermal titillation – that it is easy to confuse them. Very few of these painters refrained from doing what was expected of them. But they must not be forgotten.

Among the works of Largillière (figs. 59 and 60) – that excellent portrait-painter in the grand manner of the age of Louis XIV – and of Perronneau (fig. 75), La Tour (fig. 81), the Coypels (figs. 72 and 73), Greuze (fig. 63–5), Vigée-Lebrun (fig. 84), Parrocel, Pater (figs. 43–8), Natoire and Gillot (who as Watteau's master should have headed the list) we must pause for a moment to study Nattier, Liotard, Moreau l'Aîné and Hubert Robert, all of whom seem to merit special attention. However, I shall content myself with a few word about each, mentioning their individual merits in so far as I can within the proportions of this study.

Moreau l'Aîné (fig. 85)

Among this last group I have chosen Moreau l'Aîné as being more sensitive than Desportes, his fellow landscape-painter at a time when 'pure landscape' was still a novelty, an exceptional rarity. But I must repeat that I am only following my own reactions and my own taste for, however impartial I try to be, my personal bias must carry the day. I will at least try to give reasons for it whenever I can. But how can one fail to notice the new life that Moreau l'Aîné infused into the landscape-painting of his day, or to see in it a prefiguration, however timid, of what it was to become in the fairly distant future? Some of his *Environs of Paris*, which anticipate the Impressionists' approach to light, invite more prolonged attention. Behind his attractive ingenuousness, we see this artist discreetly heralding the nineteenth-century cult of the 'open air'. This same open air, but less tremulous and also less subjective, is to be found in the background of Hubert Robert's works, which have also other virtues to interest us.

Hubert Robert (figs. 55–8)

Hubert Robert's function as an excellent decorator, and his taste for ruins – just beginning to be discovered and appreciated by his century (Herculaneum and Pompeii had recently been excavated) – earn him a special place and give his work its marked character. We must not forget that Roman ruins had already inspired Piranesi's splendid and hallucinatory engravings, which were beginning to be known all over Europe. But Hubert Robert's vision was more modest and more tender. And his ruins, framed and also rejuvenated by the surrounding landscapes, were above all serving his purpose as a decorator. His work had undoubted merits and one can but pay homage to this lover of trees, and to his robust or delicate drawings of them, often reminiscent of Fragonard's admirable sanguines of marvellous rustling foliage. Again, he was well aware how to unite the mineral kingdom, as it might be found haunting a dream of Baudelaire's, with 'vegetable disorder'. But his inspiration was essentially decorative and faithful to nature; a present-day tree casts its shadow over the temples of the past. Whereas his subjects might have led to the introduction of mythology – in the eighteenth century satyrs and nymphs were introduced into worldly society as a means of evoking libertine ideas – Hubert Robert described only what he saw: real individuals inhabiting and traversing landscapes and sites, and already suggesting a very modern nostalgia for travel.

Nattier (fig. 67)

For Nattier, mythology was merely a useful pretext. A colourist who was privileged to invent and give his name to a blue, he borrowed goddesses' names and the allegories they illustrated. This enabled him to portray the Court beauties in simple clothes. He could airily disrobe his models without offence to decency, although such a precaution hardly seems necessary in the century we are considering. Even the sisters of King Louis the Well-Beloved willingly displayed themselves thus transformed into Venus or Diana. But we are concerned with the artist's undoubted talent, the firmness of his drawing, his happy combinations of colour. He is distinguished among his innumerable fellow-painters by the serious and unaffected elegance of his brushwork, the natural grace of his poses and compositions, the relaxed happiness expressed by his work, and the delectable quality of his paint. If most of the artists of his day strove to please at any price, Nattier succeeded in doing so without having recourse to any musty formula, but by means of a natural gift which was closely connected (it must be emphasized) with his genuine and enchanting qualities as a painter. No one succeeds in being charming, graceful and seductive by means of effort and stratagem, and such an attempt is all the more to be condemned because it cannot achieve his aim.

Liotard (figs. 154 and 155)

The same virtue of sincerity emanates from the work of Liotard, 'the Genevan' as he was called, though he came of French stock. But his striking originality must be mentioned. It may be due, as is sometimes lightly affirmed, to the fact that he refreshed his vision by his journey to the Orient, and to Constantinople in particular, but it seems more likely that it was inherent in him. Of course the subjects he chose brought out and emphasized it. He knew how to make the most of them by means of his tireless curiosity and any methods suggested to him by his craft. If he handles oils in an individual manner, allowing his subtlety and delicacy as a colourist to blossom freely, the difficult technique of pastel is just as dear to him. In this domain also he only follows the dictates of his own experience. His execution always manifests a quality of extreme simplicity which is in itself a triumph. One finds it in his direct and naturalistic portraits, some of them little short of perfection; one finds it also in sober still-lifes that amaze by their very elimination of picturesque excess. And the Oriental garb he made his models wear adds to the sense of the unexpected, of a happy surprise, that he communicates. These charming 'Turkish' paintings naturally make one think of the spread of the taste for Oriental subjects during the nineteenth century – of Delacroix, Decamps, and their numerous following ending with Gauguin . . .

Oudry (figs. 76 and 77)

Room must be found for Oudry in these pages. Some at least of his researches are of interest to his fellow-artists. They are mainly concerned with purely pictorial problems, especially those which confront the artist in the realm of *colour-values*. If I have dinned this phrase into the reader's ears, I assure him I have a reason for it.

It is interesting to note that it was the portrait-painter Largillière who drew Oudry's attention to a subject which – it goes without saying – is in the forefront of any true painter's preoccupations. It was he who revealed to Oudry the technique of rendering or translating the particular whiteness of silver objects. He gave him a recipe for the purpose whose ingenuity cannot fail to astonish the layman: namely, to surround the objects in question with others just as white but made of *different materials*. Napkins and china, stuffs and pottery would have the effect of bringing out by means of comparison and contrast the peculiar whiteness of silverware.

Oudry was marvellously receptive to the subtle technique confided to him by the portrait-painter, and he set to work with passionate concentration. The result was one of the most famous of still-lifes. It represents a duck with a candle-stick (and of course a candle) beside it, the composition completed by a table-cloth displaying its special whiteness, and a square piece of paper with the artist's signature on it. Diderot stopped before this work for a brief moment, and barely mentioned it; but it has delighted more than one real connoisseur, and some time later Oudry renewed the attempt with other themes. This description of his 'symphonies in different whites', to paraphrase Théophile Gautier's poem, is not introduced casually here. I have lingered beside them because they are deeply concerned with the art of painting. Though reduced to the apparently modest proportions of a technical problem, they exemplify one of the cardinal rules of the colourist's science.

By his delicate differentiation between whites Oudry, the painter of hunting-scenes and animals, illustrates in the clearest fashion the essential qualities required to be a painter in the pure meaning of the word. I hope to be forgiven this technical passage, which I believe to be necessary to the understanding of an art certain of whose fundamental laws – particularly the one I have just expounded – are never mentioned or analysed by the great majority of writers on painting. It is nevertheless of capital importance. It is thanks to such a perception of nuances, of colour-values – an acute, an exceptional perception – that the visible world can be modelled; and it is thanks to this perception that Chardin, Corot and Vermeer have reached the eminence they occupy and achieved their incomparable greatness.

David (fig. 86)

By tradition David must be included here, though in fact he merely symbolizes a reaction against eighteenth-century art. He has nothing in common with the painting whose systematic characteristics we have just emphasized – priority of elegance, exaggeration of pleasure, an optimistic vision of life – painting that depended on the Court, on an aristocracy for whom the only thing that counted was facile happiness and perpetual diversion. Of course, this assumed yet fanatical sensuality had certain good results, particularly in stimulating the quest for agreeable, appetizing colour of real quality. This emanated naturally enough from that valuable source of chromatic power, the north – including of course the north of Italy, Venice, the true capital of symphonies in colour.

But the use of *fêtes* as themes did not multiply indefinitely; 'the religion of Aristippus' (the apostle of pleasure for its own sake) finally engendered a state of lassitude and, as the history of art consists almost entirely of reactions, a swing of the pendulum at last reversed the seemingly perpetual laws of fashion. Now came a return to form, to austere, serious and noble historical subjects. In them we find that a more rigorous draughtsmanship aims at occupying the first place. Antiquity is of necessity the model, with its plastic universe ruled by line: in a word, all roads led to Rome at this time. David started this revolution in painting at the very moment when the heavy tread of the French Revolution began to be heard through the gay but exhausted music which was still lulling the slumbers of the tottering monarchy.

It is with some regret that I bring to an end our stroll beside the long frieze of the French eighteenth century. I would have preferred to omit no one of importance, even if I felt he merited disapproval. But I have refrained from expressing my lack of appeciation for the much-loved, flattered and acclaimed Greuze, in front of whose works Diderot became positively ecstatic and declared that painting ought always to point a moral. This preposterous point of view is not what astonishes me. I must repeat once again that true art, art that is valid and great and worthy of the name, makes one *forget* the subject, makes it disappear so to speak, in its own favour. Behind the condemnation of the *theme*, so dear to modern aestheticians, lies a secret and profound cause which no one has the courage to reveal, and in fact *no one ever mentions it.* What lies hidden behind the revolt of modern art against academic art and the moribund disciplines of the nineteenth century, a revolt which even led to the creation of a new *salon*, that of the rejected? Merely the ignorance, decay and weakness shown by a once influential science and skill, which the official school could no longer transmit.

However, there was one man who tried to recover this important skill, and succeeded: the genius Delacroix. The dramatic victory of the last great European painter bears witness to the fact.

Of course the subject has no independent existence – that is a truth of the first importance. If Greuze's *The Village Bride* (fig. 64) and *A Father's Curse* are dead works and deserve to be, this is not due to their themes, but to his treatment of them. It is because genius, or even talent, is cruelly lacking in these works of Greuze, and their success is due only to the dim, theatrical anecdotes they represent. To illustrate this point, let us try to imagine for a moment what *The Entry of the Crusaders into Jerusalem* would have been like if treated by the painter of *The Broken Pitcher*. The subject, in fact, is only a pretext, and no one thinks about Venus when he stands in front of Titian's paintings in the Uffizi or the Prado. Who is concerned with Bathsheba when he looks at Rembrandt's masterpiece, that regal treasure of the Louvre? And does anyone understand the meaning of one of the most finished masterpieces in the world, *The Night Watch*, or what it represents?

Yes, indeed, the subject of a work of art matters very little or not at all, unless it is dominated and *conquered* so to speak, transformed, transfigured and metamorphosed into a work which goes beyond it in conception and style. It is the alchemist who is all-important, and the quality of the transmutation he has effected, so that nothing remains in his crucible or on his canvas but the pure gold of formal and chromatic qualities, their elements blended and completed in a homogeneous whole. This is exactly what Watteau and Chardin achieved, each with the themes his special genius selected, and this is why they were the salvation of French eighteenth-century painting.

Guardi *(figs. 107–18)*

Guardi must be approached with caution. Above all, we must set aside all conventional epithets when we try to characterize, define and understand him and his place in the history of landscape-painting, or rather in what might be called the reign of atmosphere, that intangible phenomenon in which Light lives, breathes and dies. Not the light that visits men's dwelling-places, cottages or palaces, but which takes its ease on high and is identified with the air we breathe, fragile and tremulous in its changing intensity, its weight, its lightness, its clarity or density, as its colours ripen. It was Guardi who discovered these secrets of the atmosphere, and subjected them to a profound analysis, with marvellous co-operation, of course, from his native city. Perhaps there is no other place where the light vibrates more richly and with greater intensity than it does in Venice. Caught as in a cage between a splendid sky and the sensitive sheets of water of her canals and her lagoon, the light is the beautiful prisoner of this marine city. The luminous flood gently descends from the vault of heaven to bathe the visible world and the mirror of the sea itself.

It is an incomparable dialogue, multiplying a thousand echoes in the form of reflections of reflections, exchanges and reverberations, in a tender, silent brilliance. A great festival is in progress there, the festival of the sun's rays, reigning from dawn to dusk according to the endless changes of a sky given over to clouds and mists, which join and separate as the wind drops or rises. A fine and sumptuous festival, taking possession of the visible world and holding sway in this floating city decked with light. Very much later, the French Impressionists in their turn were to discover the magic of light and how to glorify it in masterly fashion. But in the end they sometimes pushed their analyses too far and too fanatically, so that they destroyed the forms themselves.

Francesco Guardi preserves a happy mean and, while translating the light that comes and goes between sky and sea, he sets out to make a sensitive study of the way it falls on the city. Venice's astonishing architecture, built of twenty different coloured stones and marbles, gains in solidity from the contrast. This apparent contradiction, this miraculous *tour de force* is the major contribution of Guardi's peculiar vision, his talent, his originality. But of course he possesses other rare qualities. And first of all I must return to one which is a particular glory of the Venetian School and which, as I have said, was present in him from the first: the primacy of colour, his thick oily paint, that vibrant enamelled surface – this, the mysterious gift of the north accepted in all naturalness by the Venetian School, is what painting owes to Guardi, to the great Venetians and some of the best Flemish painters. It is not surprising that Guardi, one of the last of the Venetian masters, should also possess a gift which, from Guariento to Carpaccio, from Giorgione to the titanic Titian, from Tintoretto to Veronese, glorifies the palette of this incomparable school. But I must be allowed to put in a word here about that masterly innovator without whom perhaps Florence would have triumphed over Venice. For it was Titian who was the creator of the Venetian miracle, whose advent was heralded by his predecessors; the triumph of those who followed him, including Guardi, was due to him. It is impossible to be silent about Guardi's great ancestor when we pay homage to him. Perhaps I shall be forgiven for leaving the eighteenth century for a moment to speak of the giant without whom His Serene Highness's Republic would not have carried off its great victory in the plastic arts, the man whom we must recognize as the father of all modern painting.

Canaletto, whose superb qualities can only be fully grasped from the museums of England, and Belotto also portrayed their native city; but they paint a static universe, so to speak, whereas Guardi's is pure movement. This superabundance of pulsating life first appears in the tiny figures peopling his *vedute*. Their manner of moving, walking, rowing, leaning forwards, turning round and talking together is so vivid and intense that they act as a 'signature', as it were, on even the least important canvases.

We must pause here for a moment, to discuss the technique by which he achieved this. There is nothing inscrutable about it, but it demands ability and deep understanding: Guardi's ability consisted in his gift of creative observation, and he possessed a deep understanding of the human body. To gain a better understanding of this, let us look at one or other of the canvases reproduced in this little book. First, *Gala Concert at*

Venice (fig. 110), from the Munich Museum, is one that most clearly reveals the painter's mastery of movement. The vast hall overflowing with musicians and dancers displays to us an astonishing number of different attitudes, all the more effective because there is nothing exaggerated or forced about them. The bows of the group of female violinists high up on the left of the canvas are hard at work. Each performer – and there are at least thirty of them – is distinguished from the rest by her posture and movement. The dancers below display a similar diversity, with the slightest possible swaying of the hips here, arching of the body or inclination of head and neck there; while in the centre of this densely coloured master-piece, a bewigged footman stands like a symbol of this exquisite and voluptuous *fête*, holding a dish of enticing looking delicacies. His attitude has been studied just as that marvellous draughtsman Degas studied the attitudes of his dancers. Tiny though it is, the figure of this manservant stands up to a rigorous analysis; his weight is all on his left foot, whereas only the tip of his right shoe rests on the ground. And the dish is held slightly to the right, counter-balancing his head which is bent in the opposite direction. The effect of this counterpoint is really superb, for the figure's apparent immobility contains within it the potentiality, so to speak, of a sort of sliding step which he is just about to make. You may be sure that however much this little figure is enlarged it will lose nothing of its severe perfection, or of the constructive skill which has distributed the various elements of its changing equilibrium with such exquisite dis-cretion. Finally, the various delicate colours of the composition are given value in a masterly fashion by the treatment of the floor. I have pored for a long time over this warm brown parquet, its unforgettably sonorous colour and the striking solidity of its almost inconceivably dense enamelled surface.

We find these splendid qualities again, intact and redoubled, when Guardi paints his beloved native city. But now it is the air itself, the quivering waves of the sea, the gondolas and palaces, the wind-blown flags and the vast expanse of sky which are modelled in paint. The repre-sentation of the Piazza di San Marco in figure 111 shows that famous square alive with people hurrying or sauntering along. We know almost the exact time when this familiar scene is taking place: the shadow of the Doge's Palace acts as a sundial and extends to the right. It must therefore be between eleven and twelve in the morning; the magician has caught and immobilized for us a Venetian morning in the eighteenth century. The rather cold light bathing the paving stones suggests the beginning of autumn: we do not hesitate for a second, it is the September air that floats over the city. Even at the risk of indulging in 'fine' writing or using sugared words, I must testify to the colour and subtlety of the light which plays the principal role in this picture. It is the colour of a pearl – a northern pearl, I would like to think – with the somewhat bluish tinge of distant skies in which soars one of those 'marvellous clouds' that Baudelaire preferred to everything else, like a triumphant, full-blown flower.

Everyone knows that most of Guardi's long, superb series of views of Venice were sold to travellers, who carried them off as souvenirs of the City of the Sea, just as nowadays, alas, we carry off a few photographs. The English were particularly delighted with them, so the chroniclers tell us, and the Président de Brosses must certainly have admired them during his celebrated sojourn at Venice. But we must remember that he who can do great things can also do lesser ones, and realize that Guardi was not only an incomparable painter of his native city. He could decorate a church in masterly style, paint an altar-piece and skilfully arrange a composition such as the magnificent *Tobias's Wedding*, achieved with his brother Antonio's collaboration. We are familiar with his accomplished and beautiful decorations (akin to Tiepolo's) such as those in the famous Palazzo Labia, or the astonishing *Miracle of Saint Hyacinth* in the Vienna Museum. Guardi knew how to conceive and carry out religious compositions or to let gods and demigods spring spontaneously from his brush in pagan scenes. But he does not fulfil himself completely in works such as these, or reveal the depth of his originality; I mention these genres as examples of his skill, his knowledge of anatomy and his very various abilities, and to explain how he was able to bring a myriad figures to life in the alleys of Venice in so masterly a way, and give them such an extraordinary appearance of vitality. And I must add once again that his finest achievement was to illuminate this delightful human anthill and its famous monuments and palaces with the beautiful light peculiar to the Doge's domain, a light that models, sculpts and chisels the masses in relief like a searchlight, whether they are buildings, architectural ornaments, sailing-boats, gondolas or their occupants. Anyone who knows this light knows the marvellous shadow that accompanies it. They divide his field of vision between them, and create a balance which weighs the innumerable aspects of the solid city of Venice resting upon its two scales. For if the sun lights up the ochre and russet of the Venetian houses, the shadows throw purplish veils over them. This chromatic transposition reveals Guardi as a great painter, brother to Chardin or Vermeer. But while these two are masters of controlled draughtsmanship, Guardi blossoms into calligraphy so personal that I cannot pass it by without comment. It is so perfectly incorporated in his painting that one does not at first distinguish its special character unless one studies his magical brushwork through a magnifying-glass. To gain an idea of it one has only to look at one of his drawings, a sketch or a pen-and-ink note for the composition of a painting. We see a calligraphy that is surprising, indeed quite extraordinary. His way of drawing is unique; it is useless to compare it to that of the most original of artists, to Tintoretto's agglomeration of circles, to the foreshortenings and haphazard or elliptical notes of draughts-men of every age: this is like none of them.

Is it possible to give some idea in words of this Venetian's lightning-swift shorthand and the deliberate, controlled tremor that characterizes it? As if seized with madness, his pen attacks the page and shudders rapidly across it. Looping, clawing, slashing, wielded by the demon of speed, sometimes winding its way like rain down a window-pane, some-times developing countless convolutions which seem to have been thrown on the paper anyhow in an inextricable network, it nevertheless pursues its aim, builds a palace, hollows out an arch, sets up columns, delineates a moving figure, and creates a marble staircase of innumerable steps with a single logically jerky stroke. Nothing escapes its restrained eloquence, and the warring reflections of buildings on the lagoon are seized and immobilized upon the shifting water. One is left dismayed by the ef-fectiveness of this fictitious disorder, and by the economy displayed in the very heart of such misleading prodigality. As a climax to this astonishing feat, we see patches of shadow thrown down among this confused maze of lines like musical chords between sheets of fermenting sunlight. It is clear that this choreography of line is controlled by an uncannily skilled hand, but that in spite of appearances Francesco Guardi was no virtuoso – it is a question of marvellous ability.

All these sheets covered with drawings, sketches and notes set down from observation, are for him no more than raw material extracted from the 'dictionary of nature', as Delacroix called it. Guardi was not anxious to display them, and his illusory virtuosity was not intended to be seen by all and sundry. A true virtuoso is an exhibitionist, whereas Guardi stored away his drawings as a bee stores nectar to make honey-combs. Finally let me say, before I leave the subject of his drawings, that he sometimes shows a mysterious resemblance to another draughtsman of genius. Look carefully at the *Piazza San Marco* in the Berlin Museum (or in his *Collected Drawings*) or else at the *Portico of the Doge's Palace*, belonging to the Horne Museum at Florence: you will at once recognize the claw-mark of the Dutch lion himself – Rembrandt.

We have come to the end of our thousand-year-long fresco of Venetian painting: Francesco Guardi, the last painter from the city of lagoons, unwittingly brought to a glorious end the long procession of the Venetian miracle, just before the final eclipse of the Doge's Republic. He it was who painted the Bucentaur, the galley of state symbolizing Venetian greatness, so soon to founder. Guardi was undoubtedly the herald announcing the advent of the open-air painters of the future – and he was himself among the greatest of them. For in spite of the relatively modest proportions of his canvases and the limitations of the subjects themselves, let us make no mistake about it: we must recognize their valuable and rare qualities, and see in him a great master. He sings of the sea and light, of the three elements rather – earth, water and fire. And how should it be otherwise? This child of the Adriatic summons up a legendary image, standing between past and future and, as a lover of his work, I must be forgiven for honouring it in these pages. He makes us think of a marvellous sea-shell. The murmur that is heard when one puts it to one's ear is no illusion. All the Venetian painting of the past is subtly echoed within. His chief triumph, colour, vibrates in the air and beneath the living sky, and is expressed in a delectable, drawn-out murmur. But if we listen to it attentively we shall perceive therein as well the far-off rising tide of modern art, to which Guardi already belongs.

Tiepolo *(figs. 89–98)*

Italian painting was advancing towards its decline during the eighteenth century. After the most prodigiously abundant harvest ever seen had enormously enriched the universal heritage of the plastic arts, it was only natural that its sources should begin to dry up. I must repeat, however, what everyone knows, that what has been called the Greek miracle was followed by only one other, in the domain of art at least, and that was the Italian miracle. No other western country has given us five centuries of uninterrupted creativeness. Italy's case is therefore unique, dazzling and inexplicable, like certain natural phenomena not yet – and perhaps never to be – fathomed by science. Not only did Italy invent the art of painting in the sense in which we understand it today, but she carried it to supreme perfection. A veritable army of artists, architects, painters, sculptors and goldsmiths is strung out over six hundred years. Italy discovered perspective, invented the science of movement and chiaroscuro, established the rules of composition, pushed the technique of drawing to unsurpassed heights, and finally, thanks chiefly to Venice, gave the world colour in all its most sumptuous vibrations.

Men like Giotto, Cimabue, Donatello and Michelangelo, da Vinci and Titian, Raphael and Masaccio, Botticelli and Mantegna, Piero della Francesca and Tintoretto, Pisanello and Fra Angelico – to mention only a handful of gods and demigods – and hundreds of others sprang from this privileged soil; and there were universal geniuses among them – da Vinci, Michelangelo and Titian – so that it seems natural enough that by the eighteenth century their country was, so to speak, out of breath. But its declining strength could still give us an enchanting decorator like Tiepolo, as well as the great artist we have just been speaking of, Francesco Guardi. Domenico, brother of the former, and Longhi, were no more than charming ghosts making their appearance just as the Republic of Venice completed a century of existence.

It is difficult to speak of Giovanni Battista (Giambattista) Tiepolo without mentioning his predecessors, particularly Veronese, from whom he certainly derived his gifts as a painter of frescoes, though he transformed Veronese's andantes into airy allegros. If he elaborates and lightens the decorative motifs, he imprints his personal vision on them in so doing. To put it more clearly, Tiepolo's evident originality was manifested in more than one way, above all in his style, but also in composition, draughtsmanship and colour. This originality is all the more striking if we call to mind what might be called the 'winged world' in his works, the floating universe he made his own. When one thinks of his work it seems as if he had illustrated better than anyone else man's mysterious, ancestral dream of being able to leave the earth, overcome the force of gravity and discover the intoxicating power of revolving in space by his own efforts. For my part I do not believe that this obsession was derived from the mere fact that he decorated ceilings. The reverse is probably true. Besides, other artists, other decorators have painted ceilings and domes without necessarily creating a universe where every living creature possesses an angel's privilege. Notice too that these vast airy regions are traversed and chanelled in the most natural way by figures unequipped with symbolic wings. Some are borne aloft on clouds. Others rest on floating fragments, which have lent them their own unsubstantiality. And one sees yet other divinities idly hovering and gliding through the air, or – more amazingly still – enthroned in the sky, their elbows gently supported on nothingness. Relieved of all weight, they traverse the inaccessible blue spaces, whose deliriously haunting quality is described in a poem of Mallarmé's. Tiepolo displays his special world to us in a series of skilful, birdlike evolutions. What a marvellous excuse for a brilliant draughtsman to put his prodigious talent for every form of perspective at the service of his peculiar lyricism – the lyricism of movement as it might be called. These heroes, gods and demigods, these clusters of divinities and cherubs, revolving, falling, jostling, somersaulting, coalescing or embarking on a vertiginous descent, impose on their creator problems of perspective which Tiepolo solves with disconcerting brilliance. It is as if he himself had performed these feats, and floated above the people who gaze up at his works, as if he had ridden through the sky, revolving as he went, like a soul set free at last to cross the winding paths of the empyrean.

He has been naively reproached for the so-called dryness and dullness of his colours, like those of gouache painting. This last epithet is the only one that is justified, even when he uses oil-paint for his decorations. But it is a serious error to fail to realize the necessity he was under of restricting himself to the matt colours used in wall-painting. They were imposed on him by the essential spirit of fresco, and the fact that he was expressing himself as a decorator.

Were Tiepolo's astonishing gifts confined to those I have described? This is far from the case, and I have still to mention one of his most important discoveries, which may have been derived from his floating world. It consists in the creation of a very individual aerial perspective which is difficult to describe. I am thinking of the depth of his heavenly space. The novelty of this can be realized if we compare it to the backgrounds of Veronese, for example, or some other decorator. If we find it comparatively easy to imagine a bottomless nadir beneath our feet, Tiepolo for his part proves to us, brush in hand, that there is no end to the profundity of the zenith. In him we find an explorer of the void, a man who knows, has experienced and taken the path which climbs towards infinity. I think there are various causes which contribute to this impression. The infinite spaces do not terrify him; they are divided up in masterly fashion by a multitude of figures of necessarily diverse proportions. But, whereas other artists are content to present us with a fixed and given depth, Tiepolo offers us depth itself. The figures, the clouds, the cherubs, the tenuous wreaths of vapour growing more indistinct the farther away they are, followed by more clouds and tiny figures, put an ever greater distance between us and the zenith we are contemplating, to such effect that our eye pierces to the heights, as it were, from star to star, driven up and up in a dizzy ascent. In this way the notion of an end is banished from our minds, and replaced by the idea of infinity. Of course, Tiepolo's colours effectively assist the magic flight, by their increasingly pale tonality. In fact we have left the earth ourselves, and are at the mercy of this triumphant Icarus.

Tiepolo's work is of unusual richness. Whether sacred or profane, it bears the imprint of his undeniable originality. In my youth I ranked him second to Veronese – a painter with very similar preoccupations as a decorator. But the passage of time has in the end proved that he was one of the pillars of Venetian painting, without, of course, producing anything to equal the masterpieces of a giant like Titian, or even Tintoretto. But Tiepolo's misleading facility, his gift for orchestrating compositions as he went along, had its effect on my appreciation of him – an optical illusion which is perhaps familiar to aestheticians of the past and even the present. Lightly touching rhetoric from afar, his eloquence is only seemingly superficial; his virtuosity, his excess of skill, his wealth of output are all inevitably connected (though one forgets this) with the fact that for technical reasons his special function as a fresco-painter entails constant improvisation. Then again, his work must almost always be seen from a distance. Yet it is from close quarters that the solid, deep-seated qualities of this born painter's works can best be seen. His portraits and easel-paintings bear witness to this. They also reveal in a most convincing manner the originality of his palette and his unconventionality, where movement and composition are concerned, not to mention his draughtsmanship, whose lightest stroke displays a profoundly personal calligraphy. Quantities of his drawings exist, and his stray sheets and sketch-books show to what extent this man who had to paint fast and improvise when he was painting a wall had studied reality, as it is called, in a completely direct way. The famous sketch-book in the Museo Correr at Venice, with its drawings in sanguine and charcoal on blue-grey paper, shows how he studied drapery for instance. The different stuffs are delineated with a brilliance hinted at in his painting, and there are faces also, vibrant with life, whose every line and shadow, roughly or delicately rubbed in, bears his imprint. This artist's natural habitat is the sky, but he draws upon the power of flight only by studying mortal life on earth. His most masterly compositions are derived from mythology and the supernatural, and we must turn to myth ourselves if we want to define his work. I have said that he succeeded where Icarus failed, but he also illustrates the legend of Antaeus. Like the Greek hero, it was only by constantly setting his feet on the earth that he reached the sky. So it was that this 'realist', this studious and attentive observer, was able in the most natural way in the world to reign over the heights of the kingdom of Legend itself.

Let us admit that it is very difficult to imagine Tiepolo making use of scaffolding and ladders to reach domes and ceilings and execute some *Rape of Andromeda*, or Perseus astride of Pegasus.

If caution has prevented my describing his rapid, exact, perpendicular flight towards the dome of our choice, it is because the clear-sighted reader has himself imagined the scene that I have tried to suggest in a whisper, by way of conclusion.

The Italian School

There were many other Italian eighteenth-century painters besides the two great artists to whom my last two sections were devoted, and I shall single out some for mention, as I did in the case of the French School. But though the Italian painters were more numerous than the French, there were fewer original artists among them. If I keep the more important to the end of the chapter, it is because they take us back to Venice, the source of all the works of most permanent value produced during the century.

I will note here the names of Conca and Batoni (fig. 133) – both born in Rome – who laboriously tried to prolong the last gleams of the Renaissance and its classicism. But the work is admittedly that of 'Roman copyists', and we shall turn to more definite personalities such as Giordano, Amigoni (fig. 134), the Bibienas, Ghislandi above all, Pannini (figs. 127 and 128), Piazzetta (fig. 131), Traversi, Ricci (fig. 132), Carriera (fig. 129), and lastly Magnasco (figs. 87 and 88) – the most interesting of the list.

Ghislandi and Pannini (figs. 127 and 128)

But before speaking of him I would like to say a few words about Ghislandi and his undoubted qualities as a portraitist. The portraits of his maturity in particular reveal a distinctive personality, in both interpretation and treatment. For instance, the audaciously characterized *Portrait of Isabella Camozzi dei Gherardi* shows that his models could not escape his penetrating observation. His style reveals an artist who makes no concessions, and his enthusiasm for paint redeems what might have been too direct, truthful and aggressive an approach to his models. But it is this frankness which gives his canvases their attractive asperity. He is represented, among other paintings, in the Museo Poldi Pezzoli at Milan by the *Gentleman in a Three-Cornered Hat*, perhaps his masterpiece. His essential qualities are here carried to the greatest possible pitch of intensity, power, and brilliance. No concession to the taste of the period, no desire to please, has tempered the work of this artist, who might be called a reactionary, so rare is this resistance to the desire to seduce and flatter in portraitists in general, but especially in those of the eighteenth century. I must also say something about Pannini, creator of historical paintings, but above all of *Vedute* in a style all his own which had a definite influence on European painting of this genre, especially in France.

Magnasco (figs. 87 and 88)

But Magnasco is undoubtedly the strangest, the most original of all these artists. It is traditional to liken him to Daumier. Apart from a palette dominated by browns, I see no profound reason for the comparison. Daumier was a great satirist and an admirable painter, but his masterly simplifications have nothing in common with Magnasco's neurotic calligraphy. On the contrary, Magnasco subjects his figures to constant, systematic distortion, giving them an indescribable air of agitation. They irresistibly suggest that they are taking part in a perpetual dance – St Vitus's dance perhaps. Their bodies, arms and legs, the folds of their clothes, even the decors surrounding them, follow the zigzag motion of lightning or Faraday's galvanic current, and make one think of the famous frog in the experiment. We have here a spasmodic form of baroque, and the originality of the style is manifest. Whether his paintings deal with pagan or sacred subjects, they are all crowded with gesticulating figures, making up a sort of jerky arabesque. Even the monks he was so fond of painting all seem to be afflicted with this restless excitement, and appear positively bewitched! He sometimes reminds one of certain of Tintoretto's compositions (rather than Daumier's), such as the masterly and fantastic *Transportation of the Body of St Mark*, or the *Macabre Scene* from the church of Santa Maria Assunta at Pavia. I must add that even apart from the all-important factor of his very personal vision, he has admirable painterly qualities. The sobriety of his palette – true painters know how to be colourists without having recourse to excessive polychromy – does not prevent his tonality from being richly varied, and the oily, thick consistency of his paint contributes to the sumptuousness of his canvases. His style certainly entitles him to a special place among the minor painters I have enumerated.

Although this work is concerned with painting alone, I find it quite impossible to pass over the name of that unequalled draughtsman and marvellous engraver Piranesi, who enriched his century with visionary works wherein the imagination of an architect who was also a magician constructed a hallucinatory world that has inspired Western artists.

Canaletto (figs. 102–6)

I must now return, as I promised, to Venice. Even if Tiepolo and Guardi tower above the other painters of the last years of the Doge's regime, we must not omit Antonio Canale, known as Canaletto, not only because he preceded Francesco Guardi in time, but also because he too portrayed the city of lagoons. He worked with careful objectivity, by which I mean that he tried to get as close as possible to what we call reality for, as everyone knows, undiluted naturalism is practically non-existent in art. Courbet made a sincere attempt at a passionate objectivity, but remained a triumphant dupe of it.

Canaletto's *Vedute* are at least the work of a faithful observer. They have been observed with an architect's eye, although his qualities as a serious painter to a large extent redeem their too severe and dry precision. The latter characteristics apply in particular to his youthful work. His stay in England, where he was much admired, introduced him to the work of the Flemish painter van der Heyden, we are told, and his technique as a colourist benefited from the contact. I have always admired this excellent painter, but it was in England that I really discovered him. It was there that Canaletto shook off, as by a miracle, that submission to the visible world which had lent his early works a documentary aspect, so that they appear to be statements so scrupulous that they sometimes resemble official reports. But he got rid of some of his naturalistic rationalism while in London and was revealed as a fine and solid painter of urban landscape. However, his personality resisted this enrichment, and his slightly chilly immobility is always visible through the new gifts that made him into a painter of real merit. Though it is unfair and almost cruel to compare him to the poetic Guardi, he was nevertheless a master of prose, with a prose style that in the course of his career gently moved in the direction of genuine interpretation. This is to be seen especially in the way he en- larged and broadened his subjects, calmly magnifying the perspectives. He was also far from ignorant of atmospheric space, and his last works, by progressively eliminating a too explicit duet between light and shade, permit the latter to invade his canvases more freely. In London one may admire works that reveal – very discreetly it is true – his debt to Guardi; they are alive with vibrations and gleams of light to which one cannot be indifferent. However, Canaletto's classicism is quite distinct and remote from Guardi's lyric song, and it never lost that somewhat fixed serenity that was to be wakened and brought to life by Guardi, as the wind disturbs a too calm sky and tears apart the tranquil clouds. Guardi's poetry put fire and movement into the visible world; it was pre-romantic, to use the word in its old sense of ardour and subjectivity.

Belotto (figs. 99–101)

I must say a few words also about the Venetian Bernardo Belotto, Canaletto's nephew and pupil. An inferior painter to his uncle and master, he succeeded in shaking off that strong influence and becoming a painter of *Vedute* in his own style. These include landscapes and architectural paintings of real quality. Though he came perilously closer than his master to the dangers of photographic documentation, he never quite succumbed to them, and he fixed certain aspects of Vienna, Dresden (fig. 180) and Warsaw on his canvas with a far from negligible authoritativeness and 'free realism'.

Pietro Longhi (figs. 122–5)

As he was a Venetian, Pietro Longhi must also be mentioned here. He was a charming, picturesque chronicler, very much appreciated by lovers of his native town, whose daily life he related not without humour. Addicts of the eighteenth-century Venetian School have plenty to say about him and will continue saying it, for it is as a faithful and amused narrator that Longhi presents us with a living image of a dentist's consulting-room (fig. 125) or of the first rhinoceros ever to land on the *pavimenti* of his native town (fig. 122). He is above all an excellent journalist, and his canvases show genuine qualities of painting.

Domenico Tiepolo (figs. 119–21)

Giovanni Domenico (Giandomenico) Tiepolo, son of the great artist, has a different claim to our interest. A fresco-painter of charming and un- bridled fantasy, he too decorated villas and palaces with wit and animation. But though at first he helped his father with his Christian or pagan paintings, he later on won his way to independence and interested himself more especially in the life of the town. An excellent observer, a skilful and delicate draughtsman, he knew how to give a racy description of the Venetian crowds, and the dawdlers watching the pantaloonery of mummers, Punch and Judy shows, acrobats or tumblers. His finest frescoes are preserved in the Ca' Rezzonico; they clearly show the artist's skilled and sensitive interpretation and the way his delicately refined colour is never allowed to neglect the exigencies of the wall on which it is painted.

Some indefinable melancholy seems to waft from these joyful, smiling scenes. Perhaps it is because they are for us Venice's last smiles; the shouts of laughter from her fêtes and carnivals are gently fading like those masks evoked by Victor Hugo to represent human emotions, disappearing over the horizon before the insidious approach of the evening of life.

Goya *(figs. 138–51)*

Goya was Janus personified. The duality of man is perfectly illustrated in him. I am not referring to the two periods into which his work can be divided: to the Goya who reflected the seductions of the eighteenth century (although his strong personality was already showing through) and that other Goya who made a sudden appearance on the canvases he painted after a severe illness at the age of nearly forty-three. For the second period itself contains a contradiction: it swings between tenderness and savagery. Though he views the female sex with deep and serious sensuality, he can also dissect it, flay it alive and plunge it into the pitiless, devastating and lurid light of old age. But with Goya we are a long way from the famous portrait, formerly attributed to Giorgione, whose red-rimmed eyes gaze out at us from the walls of the Accademia at Venice. It portrays an old woman holding a banner on which are written the bitter words '*Col tempo*'. It is not only the activities of Chronos that Goya finds cruel. He does not choose a face to ravage at random. The faces he selects are already monsters of ugliness, and must have been as horrifying in their youth in a different sense as they are in their natural decline. But when he paints a young woman, his Spanish blood makes him entirely and passionately her slave. He endows her with intense attractiveness and an inward sensuality, such as we see in his *Maja Vestida*, a far more disturbing picture than his *Maja Desnuda* (fig. 149) whose conscious lasciviousness misses its aim. The important thing however is that we have here two superb paintings. And if I have lingered a moment to compare their sensuality, it is to set it against that of English or French painters who offer us either brazen lust or skin-deep sensuality instead of the feminine seductiveness of Goya's models.

This may seem an unexpected and bizarre comparison with which to begin my short study of Goya. Nevertheless it was deliberate. It emphasizes a fact and illustrates something that needs to be clarified: as I said in my Introduction, in spite of his dates the great Madrid painter does not belong to his century or to the spirit of his century – except perhaps to the very beginning of it – and I must insist that his genius is very difficult to relate to time and particularly to his own times. I also said that he was hurrying towards the future. What does that mean? Do I propose to drone out those everlasting and facile clichés claiming every great artist as a 'forerunner'? It is one of the bad habits of modern writers on art. It is true of some artists. But at the risk of paradox I would like to say that if he was a forerunner it was because of his followers . . . There have been great innovators who had no following. And why is this? Because they were so original that they could not be imitated. That is why certain artists found schools and become leaders of a group, while others remain in isolation. As examples of the latter, I will choose almost at random two very dissimilar artists known to everyone – El Greco and Brueghel. Neither of them founded a school, but each created a startlingly original style totally different from that of the other. Perhaps one can also make distinctions among those painters who collect disciples around them. While the influence of Titian or Rembrandt lasted for many years, there have been other 'giants' whose imitators have only survived them for a very short space. There is no doubt that the influence of Goya's technique and style has been long-lasting. We know what Manet and Daumier owed to him. Each was inspired by a single facet of that complex Spanish personality, itself a reflection of the sovereign lesson taught by Velázquez – for every child must have a father. Let me say, in this connection, that the naturalism, the flagrant realism which is permanently connected with Iberian painting – except for the visionary El Greco – is perhaps responsible for the fact that Goya's series of imaginative works is for the most part a distortion of this objectivity in the form of caricature. This is perhaps why neither he nor Velázquez ever to my mind really 'left the earth' to give us work that could be called sacred, for Spanish religious painting is always imprisoned in the real and visible world. And it is interesting to notice how the three Christs of Velázquez, Goya and Manet (who was influenced by them) are all strictly naturalistic. If we want sacred painting with all its other-worldly implications, we must look to Italy or other countries where it was understood, or to the great Dutchman, Rembrandt, to whom everything was possible.

And it is curious to notice even in Goya, whose work includes an irrational element, that it is never in religious painting that he becomes unrealistic. The source of his visions is to be found at the opposite pole from the divine, although it might be maintained without paradox that the Devil belongs to the world of theology. However that may be, whenever Goya abandoned reality in every form (including his admirable portraits) as he did periodically, it was certainly under the Devil's aegis. The famous canvas of the Prince of Darkness imparting his 'doctrine' to a subservient and grimacing crowd is an illustration in point. We know also how he delighted in creating his witches and warlocks and his whole world of crawling monsters. He certainly saw Bosch's Flemish devilries in the Escurial, but though these are full of a sort of infernal humour they seem to have been inspired by some bogy-man for adults. In contrast to Bosch's satanic and grotesque world of macabre, nightmare fantasy never far removed from childish buffoonery, Goya's kingdom seems like a caricature of Hell itself. It has been thought that the occupation of his country by Napoleon's armies – an occupation which never led to conquest – and the terrifying scenes he witnessed may have sharpened his bitter and violent feelings of revolt. So many bloody incidents, so many scenes of repeated and horrifying atrocity might perhaps have stimulated his powerful imagination in this nightmarish direction. But the more one looks at this explanation the less satisfactory it appears. Although some of his works depict the horrors of war, these have nothing in common with the many examples of the fantastic he has left us. What connection is there between the cruelties unfortunately involved in all wars with that strange kingdom of floating, contorted, grimacing figures who seem to belong to some witches' sabbath? This world of monsters and witches is in fact a world apart. People of keen intelligence have minutely studied 'Goya's case' as it might be called, but I must admit that none of their analyses is completely convincing. What seems certain is that the supernatural only made its appearance in the painter's works after his illness and after he had been struck with incurable deafness.

I have listened with great attention to the remarks of a perceptive young woman of remarkable intuitive powers. She made the disturbing suggestion that the noisy deafness which surrounded the great artist might have been the origin of his strange imagery. The incoherent tumult produced by his afflicted sense of hearing might, on this view, have found an outlet by entrusting to his visual sense the task of transferring it to his canvases.

However that may be, we are primarily concerned here with the qualities of Goya's work. My point of view will probably astonish and disappoint the reader and particularly the art critics, for it is very far from theirs. It will be better understood by remembering that it is above all a painter's point of view. For me, Goya's genius and his amazing personality are closely connected with the marvellous gifts he showed as a harmonist, a musician in colour, whenever he was inspired to re-create reality. Though this reality is merely a pretext, as is always the case with great masters, it must all the same be present. Goya never seems to me greater than when his work springs from what he has seen, observed, and snatched from the visible world, whether directly or through the medium of his creative memory. How is it possible to leave the visible world – to interpret it – if it is not first experienced? And in spite of the undeniable and superb qualities of his imaginary, supernatural kingdom it is to my eyes inferior to the other. Ardent admirer though I am of the fantastic in literature, I am ill at ease with it, or at least very critical of it, when expressed in form and colour. Goya is exceptional in that he preserves his painterly qualities intact even when he is depicting an unreal kingdom – it is a very rare quality indeed. Another reason for the personal uneasiness caused me by Goya's fantasias is that they are more painful than convincing. Some forced and exaggerated quality in them keeps one outside the magic circle he is tracing. Furthermore, his formal qualities, his gift of modelling a face or a body, become definitely weaker and less remarkable when he is translating his jeering visions for us. Perhaps, after all, it is impossible for a Latin to invoke the Devil. That would be more appropriate, I think, to the age of Schongauer or Dürer in Germany. One has only to think of *The Four Horsemen of the Apocalypse* to realize that Lucifer – or Sammael, the angel of Poison – his pomps and all his works, are more effective when conjured up by a Germanic eye, and that Schongauer's witches savour of heresy in a different way from those of the great Spaniard.

Goya does not depend on the 'visionary' element in his work for his place in the history of art, though it does of course complete his portrait as a man and illustrate the tragic side of his life. It is above all his portraits of groups or individuals, his frescoes (particularly those in the church of San Antonio de la Florida in Madrid) his scenes of the Napoleonic occupation and the Spanish Revolution and his marvellous still-lifes that make him a great master – not to mention the treasures of draughtsmanship which add their radiance to the picture of his art I am trying to draw.

The magic technique that has given us so many masterpieces is very much his own, yet the term 'technique' is hardly adequate to convey his manner of translating nature and embodying his vision on his canvas. But how else can one express the fact that the transposing eye and the hand that carried out the transposition bridge over the act of creation? Thus it is that a poor modern artist may scrutinize Velázquez's *Meninas* and try to discover how the miracle 'was performed', whereas the mystery really consists in the way it 'was seen'. Therein lies a poet's gift, in the etymological sense of the word. I have turned to Velázquez, whom Goya studied so deeply, because the latter sometimes reminds us of that incomparable master. The portrait of *The Condesa del Carpio, Marquesa de la Solana* (fig. 138) in the Louvre is a signal example. Here, as in the *Portrait of the Family of Carlos IV* and many others, we see Goya's supreme artistry. The Condesa del Carpio is silhouetted against a background of a single wash of paint, as Goya liked to place his models. A supremely restrained delicacy, which has nothing to do with taste but seems to belong to music alone, is the basis of this masterpiece of harmony. 'The unexpected charm of a pink and black jewel' – this well known line, dedicated by Baudelaire to Manet's model Lola de Valence, perfectly describes the two chief colours of this masterpiece. The huge bow in the sitter's hair is a pale rose-madder, while the mantilla that falls from her hair on to the long shadowy dress is a subtle grey. No concession has been made in the treatment of the face; it is modelled with magic skill, as are the two gloved hands, the fan and the dancing-shoes elegantly supporting the sitter's light and expressively feminine weight. And the background sings on exactly the right note, as in the work of all great masters. All Goya's art, his marvellously simplified complexity, his rare gifts as a 'pure' painter, his desire to tell the truth have been poured out together here in masterly fashion. We recognize the work of a great artist, for art's highest achievement is to overcome every danger: Goya has not sacrificed character to grace, he remains robust when he is seductive, he avoids over-sweetness by his restraint, he treats a dangerously pleasing subject without letting the danger be apparent, and finally he has achieved style, his own style, without exaggeration nor outrage to form. Here, in fact, we see that supreme quality – all the more remarkable in the case of so tormented a genius – a sense of proportion.

As for his marvellous world of grimacing witches, his Sabbath scenes, let us respectfully leave this mine to be explored by the literary commentators with their learned expositions.

The English School

A distinguished art historian, Tancred Borenius (Professor of History of Art, University College, London*), has told us categorically that 'the eighteenth century deserves to be ranked as one of the greatest periods of English painting'. This singularly revealing statement tells us what in fact we know already, that the nation which has given western Europe its greatest poets and novelists is undeniably poor in relation to the rest of Europe where the plastic arts are concerned. But I must here emphasize the fact that by a sort of marvellous accident – the phrase is not so exaggerated as it seems – nineteenth-century Great Britain provided us with two, if not three very important painters, two of whom were genuine innovators and had a far-reaching influence on Western art. I am speaking of that astonishing landscape-painter, Constable, and of Turner and

* In *English Painting in the Eighteenth Century* (Hyperion, 1938)

Bonington. Everyone knows how much Delacroix owed to Constable, and what a marvellous inspiration these English landscape-painters were to the new school of French painting in the nineteenth century – an inspiration which still has repercussions today! Constable's influence is an extraordinary phenomenon, one of the most unaccountable in the history of art; its consequences still amaze us.

After paying this sincere and well-deserved tribute to England I think I am entitled to criticize her artistic output during the eighteenth century with perfect freedom, especially considering the general inferiority of this period in the history of the plastic arts.

Three foreign painters established themselves in England during the seventeenth and eighteenth centuries, and exerted a considerable influence on English painting. The most important was van Dyck. We must remember that he was a portrait-painter, and that (except for a few good landscape-painters) portraiture was the chosen genre of most English artists, to which they systematically adhered and of which they produced an abundance of paintings which were naturally not free from monotony. We should be easily consoled for this – not forgetting that, as I have said more than once, the genre and subject of painting are only of secondary importance – if this army of portrait-painters were not for the most part composed of superficial virtuosos. I have applied these last two terms to eighteenth-century art in general, but it was in England that we find the most extreme instances. The insipidity, affectation and usually conventional style, the innumerable artifices resorted to by these *Court painters*, as they might be called, found the soil of this gentle and sentimental country disastrously fertile. It is useless to analyse the reasons for this; we should certainly not discover them. It is enough to know that England did not understand the plastic language. It seems that she substituted for it the language of poetry and literature, which was natural to her, and which necessarily has no place in painting though it sometimes forces an entry. Hence the species of aberration or misdirection causing artists – some of whom were talented, particularly in the use of colour – to use it to the detriment of form. This gave rise to works that were often striking, always unequal, lacking balance, and above all cruelly devoid of bony structure. I propose to illustrate this statement with examples.

To begin with let me say that English eighteenth-century art was powerfully influenced by a painter of Flemish origin – van Dyck. It must be admitted that he only belongs to the second rank in comparison to the best painters of his native land. And he was, besides, a specialist in portraiture – a painter of formal, fashionable portraits.

It was ill luck for English painting that it embarked upon the eighteenth century with van Dyck for ideal and model. It is true that later on Reynolds and Gainsborough were to study great masters like Rubens, Titian and

Rembrandt. However, in spite of such happy relationships, none of the great qualities of these masters were assimilated, realized or fully understood by their admirers. The latter were responsive mainly to the outer shell of their work, the quality of their paint or colours, without ever trying to take possession of nature, and attempt to translate or transpose it through their own experience.

Hogarth (figs. 159–61)

Hogarth's name must, of course, head the long list. It is significant that this 'genre' painter already displayed the characteristics of what was later on, and is still to this day, described as English humour, of which indeed he seems to have been the ancestor. We know that the most gifted caricaturists came from Great Britain, a country that has always shown a vocation for this form of art. But Hogarth is also in my view the most original English painter of the eighteenth century; not only in his themes but in his genuine painterly qualities. His famous *Shrimp Girl* typifies these qualities and is the work which most clearly proclaims his gifts as a painter. And in this connection I must mention that it is in his least finished works that Hogarth shows his potentialities most clearly. It is when he improvises and gets carried away by his subject that he avoids a certain dryness of approach tending to too much attention to detail, a danger that besets many painters who confuse 'finishing' with 'completing' a picture. Baudelaire gave a masterly definition of the distinction between the two when he explained – I am quoting from memory – that a picture can be finished without being completed, the first word implying a pointless fussiness whereas the completion of a work of art goes beyond detail, or may even involve its omission, and is carried out in a bold, simple style corresponding to a masterly synthesis such as we may see in a Velázquez for example.

If I were to name even the majority of English painters of the eighteenth century the list would be impressive but quite useless. I will confine myself therefore to the names most representative of this school. After Hogarth must come those of Reynolds (figs. 162–4), Gainsborough (figs. 167–9), Hoppner (fig. 174), Opie ,Raeburn (figs. 170 and 171), Romney, the caricaturist Rowlandson (fig. 175), Stubbs and finally Blake (fig. 176). But of these, Reynolds and Gainsborough are in a higher rank, along with Füssli (figs. 156–8), whose strange personality and themes set him categorically apart from his colleagues.

Reynolds (figs. 162–4)

Reynolds must come first. Even with the reservations I shall make about his work, he still remains the least weak, the most self-assured among the large family of his country's painters. Of course he was a portraitist, like all the chief painters of the English School, but he carried out his function more confidently and with more vigour. But what I have reiterated about the whole eighteenth-century English School is true of him also: in spite of the undoubted superiority of his gifts one detects in this excellent portrait-painter – though less obviously than in his colleagues, and not at first glance – a weakness in what might be called the 'backbone' of his work. In spite of his great virtues as a colourist and his respect for form, we find here and there little islands of uncertainty, secret hesitations that are purely plastic. Even my pen reflects this uncertainty, for of course it is not to be found in all Reynolds's work; nevertheless it is revealed in the majority of his canvases. There are works signed by him which tell another story, such as the portrait of Lord Heathfield, or (even more) that of the Duke of Gloucester, in the collection of my lamented friend Alex Shaw at Buenos Aires. His gift for composition is often evident, for instance in the famous portrait of Nelly O'Brien in the Wallace Collection; but even in his best canvases we always find brushwork that is an imitation, sometimes a skilful one, of that of the great Continental masters. It is not easy to define this term 'imitation', I will only say that his brushwork lacks spontaneity and seems to be the result of a triturative process full of reminiscences, and that it suggests that he is carrying out a recipe. We shall find this weakness to a more marked degree in Gainsborough, even more in the works of Romney and above all in those of the exasperating Lawrence. But the most serious and sweeping criticism that can be made of all these artists is that the figures in their portraits – clothes, arms, and stuffs – either seem made of cardboard or alarmingly insubstantial: here is a sleeve showing no trace of the arm it covers, and there a leg that looks as heavy as lead. And I must add that most of the paintings keep to certain conventions – a languid gaze, hands too gracefully clasped, an air of prefabricated charm – which sometimes, as in the case of Lawrence, are very hard to bear. Of course, one often finds pleasant colour-combinations, but they reveal taste rather than real painting.

Gainsborough (figs. 167–9)

Reynolds's true and only rival, though his inferior, Gainsborough has real charm and his landscapes, in the backgrounds of his portraits, are greater and more important. We owe to that particular taste numerous paintings of which the landscape is the dominant feature; both the Dutch and, supremely Claude Lorrain have benefited from this influence.

Füssli (figs. 156–8)

I must here mention an 'English' painter of Swiss origin, who has nothing in common with the English School or even with the art of his century, any more than the fantastic Goya had with his. I mean Füssli, a difficult personality to describe, and one who makes one think of Achim von Arnim, Hoffmann, Poe, or any other teller of 'uncanny tales' concerning dreams and hallucinations. He displays a hectic pre-romanticism, probably closer to the German visionaries than to the great American poet whose macabre and splendid phantoms obey the laws of an inspired rationalism. All this implies that Füssli belongs more to literature than to the world of the plastic arts, which is far from laudatory comment. However, his work involves qualities of composition, ideas and often colour and form which cannot be passed over in silence, although his paint has the en-amelled appearance typical of eighteenth-century English painting. It must be admitted that it is with surprise rather than pleasure that, after a procession of fashionable portraits, we suddenly come across one of his monsters, spawned by Night and wreathed in smoke, with eyes that seem to belong to the world of magic. After Füssli we must make a note of Blake, who also tried to translate his poetic visions, mainly in terms of watercolour and drawing. But his literary achievement gave final and valid expression to a world foreign to the plastic arts.

The long procession of English painters will not gain from a more detailed study, and the mere fact of mentioning other artists would only cause useless duplication. I will end by repeating the truth revealed by our general study of the English School. England is the country where words and song reigned supreme, but it was unfavourable soil to formal values, whether in architecture, sculpture, painting or drawing. Among her 'great eighteenth-century painters,' those most gifted as colourists never achieved their aim: their lack of sense of form impeded them and interfered with their chromatic talent. There was a mysterious fatality about it. Though there were one or two good landscape-painters or skilled and careful animal-painters among them, these hardly alter the picture of the eighteenth-century that I have attempted to outline for you. But we must not forget that we have only to wait for the following century if we want to do homage to the plastic art of this country. Then we shall honour that great, inventive landscape-painter Constable, made greater still by his amazing influence on the Continent; and beside him stands Turner, an astonishing visionary in spite of the relative insubstantiality of his poetical mirages. And lastly, we must not forget that sober, subtle and remarkable landscape-painter, Bonington.

Eighteenth-Century Painting

Illustrations

1 Antoine Watteau

2 Antoine Watteau

3   Antoine Watteau

4 Antoine Watteau

5　Antoine Watteau

6 Antoine Watteau

7 Antoine Watteau

8 Antoine Watteau

9 Antoine Watteau

10 Antoine Watteau

11 Antoine Watteau

12 Antoine Watteau

13 Antoine Watteau

14　Jean-Baptiste-Siméon Chardin

15   Jean-Baptiste-Siméon Chardin

16 Jean-Baptiste-Siméon Chardin

17 Jean-Baptiste-Siméon Chardin

18   Jean-Baptiste-Siméon Chardin

19   Jean-Baptiste-Siméon Chardin

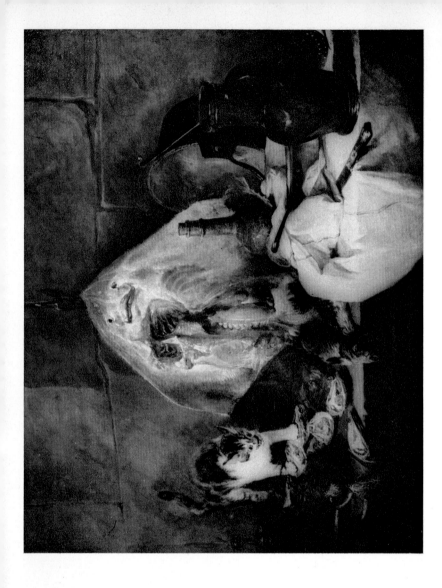

20 Jean-Baptiste-Siméon Chardin

21   Jean-Baptiste-Siméon Chardin

22 Jean-Baptiste-Siméon Chardin

23   Jean-Baptiste-Siméon Chardin

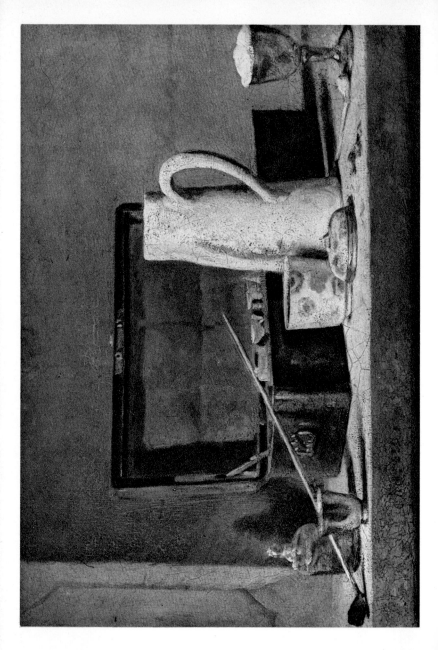

24   Jean-Baptiste-Siméon Chardin

25   Jean-Baptiste-Siméon Chardin

26   Jean-Honoré Fragonard

27   Jean-Honoré Fragonard

28　Jean-Honoré Fragonard

29   Jean-Honoré Fragonard

30　Jean-Honoré Fragonard

31 Jean-Honoré Fragonard

32   Jean-Honoré Fragonard

33 Jean-Honoré Fragonard

34 Jean-Honoré Fragonard

35   Nicolas Lancret

36 Nicolas Lancret

37 Nicolas Lancret

38 Nicolas Lancret

39   Nicolas Lancret

40 Nicolas Lancret

41 Nicolas Lancret

42   Nicolas Lancret

43   Jean-Baptiste Pater

44   Jean-Baptiste Pater

45　Jean-Baptiste Pater

46   Jean-Baptiste Pater

47 Jean-Baptiste Pater

48   Jean-Baptiste Pater

49 François Boucher

50 François Boucher

51   François Boucher

52 François Boucher

53 François Boucher

54 François Boucher

55 Hubert Robert

56 Hubert Robert

57   Hubert Robert

58 Hubert Robert

59　Nicolas de Largillière

60 Nicolas de Largillière

61   Hyacinthe Rigaud

62　Hyacinthe Rigaud

63   Jean-Baptiste Greuze

64   Jean-Baptiste Greuze

65 Jean-Baptiste Greuze

66 Claude-Joseph Vernet

67 Jean-Marc Nattier

68   Alexandre-François Desportes

69 François-Hubert Drouais

70   François-Hubert Drouais

71 Joseph-Siffrède Duplessis

72 Noël-Nicolas Coypel

73 Antoine Coypel

74   Alexis-Simon Belle

75 Jean-Baptiste Perronneau

76 Jean-Baptiste Oudry

DOMINA MARIA IOSEPHE DRUMMOND COMITISSA...
...ISSIMVS POTENTISSIMVS NEC...
NON NOBILISSIMVS PRINCEPS...
DRVMMOND DVISDE MELFORT...
...PVTICILERES ORDINIS EQVITIS...

77   Jean-Baptiste Oudry

78 Louis-Michel Vanloo

79 Pierre-Paul Prud'hon

80 Louis Tocqué

81 Maurice-Quentin de La Tour

82 Jean-François de Troy

83 Claude Gillot

84 Elisabeth-Louise Vigée-Lebrun

85 Louis-Gabriel Moreau

À MARAT.
DAVID.

86   Jacques-Louis David

87 Alessandro Magnasco

88 Alessandro Magnasco

89 Giambattista Tiepolo

90 Giambattista Tiepolo

91 Giambattista Tiepolo

92 Giambattista Tiepolo

93 Giambattista Tiepolo

94 Giambattista Tiepolo

95 Giambattista Tiepolo

96 Giambattista Tiepolo

97 Giambattista Tiepolo

98 Giambattista Tiepolo

99 Bernardo Belotto

100   Bernardo Belotto

101 Bernardo Belotto

103　Canaletto

104 Canaletto

105 Canaletto

106 Canaletto

107 Francesco Guardi

108   Francesco Guardi

109 Francesco Guardi

110 Francesco Guardi

111 Francesco Guardi

112 Francesco Guardi

113　Francesco Guardi

114 Francesco Guardi

115 Francesco Guardi

116 Francesco Guardi

117 Francesco Guardi

118 Francesco Guardi

119 Giandomenico Tiepolo

120　Giandomenico Tiepolo

121 Giandomenico Tiepolo

Within the painting, inscription on placard:

Vero Ritratto
Di un Rinoceronte
Condoto in Venezia
l'Anno 1751
Fatto per mano di
Pietro Longhi
per Commissione
del N.H. Giovanni Grimani
dei Servi Patrizio Veneto

122   Pietro Longhi

123   Pietro Longhi

124 Pietro Longhi

125   Pietro Longhi

126   Alessandro Longhi

127 Giovanni Paolo Pannini

128 Giovanni Paolo Pannini

129 Rosalba Carriera

130 Giambattista Pittoni

131　Giovanni Battista Piazzetta

132 Sebastiano Ricci

133 Pompeo Batoni

134　Jacopo Amigoni

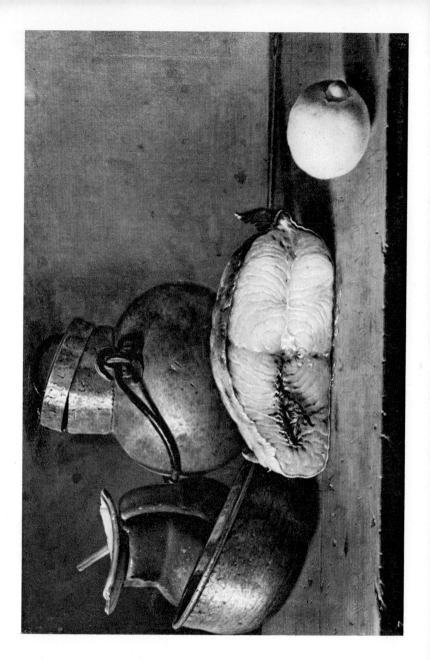

135 Luis Eugenio Meléndez

136   Luis Paret y Alcázar

137 Anton Raphael Mengs

138 Fráncisco de Goya

139 Francisco de Goya

140   Francisco de Goya

141 Francisco de Goya

142 Francisco de Goya

143 Francisco de Goya

144   Francisco de Goya

145 Francisco de Goya

146   Francisco de Goya

147 Francisco de Goya

148 Francisco de Goya

149 Francisco de Goya

150 Francisco de Goya

151 Francisco de Goya

152   Cornelis Troost

153 Franz Anton Maulbertsch

154 Jean-Etienne Liotard

155   Jean-Etienne Liotard

156 Johann Heinrich Füssli

157   Johann Heinrich Füssli

158   Johann Heinrich Füssli

159 William Hogarth

160 William Hogarth

161 William Hogarth

162 Sir Joshua Reynolds

163   Sir Joshua Reynolds

164 Sir Joshua Reynolds

165　Sir Thomas Lawrence

166 Sir Thomas Lawrence

167　Thomas Gainsborough

168 Thomas Gainsborough

169 Thomas Gainsborough

170 Henry Raeburn

171 Henry Raeburn

172 Richard Wilson

173　John Crome

174 John Hoppner

175 Thomas Rowlandson

176　William Blake

Biographical Notes

Amigoni, Jacopo. An Italian painter and engraver, born in Venice in 1675, who produced altarpieces, history pieces, decorative cycles and portraits in a lively, pretty Venetian Rococo style in which the influence of Sebastiano Ricci, French Rococo masters and Tiepolo may be discerned. Successful, both in his native Venice and in London, which he visited 1730–9. In 1747 went to Spain as Court Painter and died in Madrid in 1752 (*fig. 134*)

Batoni, Pompeo. Italian painter, born in Lucca in 1708. Greatly admired Raphael and antique art but is chiefly remembered not for his rather insipid religious and mythological paintings, but for the long series of portraits he produced of visitors to Rome, often English noblemen on the Grand Tour. Died in Rome in 1787 (*fig. 133*)

Belle, Alexis-Simon. French portrait painter, born in 1674. Was a pupil of Jean François de Troy and worked for the Courts of France, Poland and England. Died in 1734 (*fig. 74*)

Belotto, Bernardo. Born in Venice in 1720, a nephew of Canaletto, under whom he trained and whose assistant he became. They separated in the early 1740s and Belotto travelled in Italy before leaving for Dresden in 1747. In 1748 he was appointed Painter to Frederick Augustus II and painted many views of Dresden, Pirna and Königstein. In the 1760s he visited St Petersburg, Vienna and Munich, settling in Poland in 1767 and becoming Court Painter to Stanislas II in 1770. Died in Warsaw in 1780. His style was based on Canaletto's but he often adopted colder colour and darker shadows. His precision was phenomenal and his views of Warsaw were of great use in the post-war rebuilding of the city (*figs. 99–101*)

Blake, William. English painter, engraver, poet and thinker, born in London in 1757. Studied at the Royal Academy Schools in the late 1770s. Most of his work is small in scale, often in water-colour and usually illustrative in character; he provided illustrations for the Book of Job and for Dante. His intensely personal vision was helped rather than hindered by undeniable formal deficiencies in his style. The weaknesses in his drawing impart a child-like intensity to his work. Died in London in 1827 (*fig. 176*)

Boucher, François. French painter, born in Paris in 1703. Studied under Le Moyne, won the Prix de Rome in 1723, went to Italy in 1727, admired the work of Tiepolo and returned to Paris in 1731. He ran a large and efficient studio which produced a stream of paintings, either to be hung independently or to be inset in panelling on walls or over doors. In 1765 he was made Painter to the King. Died in Paris in 1770 (*figs. 49–54*)

Canaletto (Antonio Canal). Italian painter, etcher and draughtsman, born in Venice in 1697. The son and pupil of Bernardo Canal, he was further influenced by the topographical work of Carlevaris and Pannini. 1746–1755 he was in England, mainly working for aristocratic patrons. After his return, his output decreased and his style became harder and his figures even more mannered. Died in Venice in 1768 (*figs. 102–6*)

Carriera, Rosalba. Italian woman painter, born in Venice in 1675. Began as a painter of allegories and mythological paintings in the Rococo style but achieved fame with her portraits in pastel. Equally successful with her contemporaries were the series of idealized, semi-erotic pastels of young girls. A very large collection of her work is at Dresden. Died in Venice in 1757 (*fig. 129*)

Chardin, Jean-Baptiste-Siméon. French painter of genre scenes, still-life and portraits, born in Paris in 1699. Studied with the history painter Cazes and Coypel, and then worked as a restorer at Fontainebleau. In the late 1720s emerged as a painter of still-life. In the 1730s began to paint genre scenes. Also produced portraits, satirical scenes with monkeys and numerous small scale still-life pieces praised by critics since Diderot. Chardin died in Paris in 1779 (*figs. 14–25*)

Coypel, Antoine. French painter, born in Paris in 1661. Was a pupil of his father, Noël-Nicolas, and became a decorative painter and designer of tapestries. Carried out several large-scale decorative commissions, including the ceiling of the Chapel at Versailles (1708). Studied in Italy, where he was influenced by Bolognese Baroque painting which he later combined with ideas taken from Rubens and Poussin. Died in Paris in 1722 (*fig. 73*)

Coypel, Noël-Nicolas. French painter, born in Paris in 1628. Worked on the decoration of the Louvre and designed tapestries and taught his more famous son, Antoine. Died in Paris in 1707 (*fig. 72*)

Crome, John. English landscape painter, known as 'Old Crome' to distinguish him from his son, born in Norwich in 1768. One of the founders of the Norwich Society in 1803 and regularly exhibited there from 1805 to 1821. Lived all his life in Norwich, where he died in 1821 (*fig. 173*)

David, Jacques-Louis. French Neo-Classical painter, born in Paris in 1748. Studied under Vien, won the Prix de Rome in 1774 and worked in Rome 1775–81. First great success was the *Oath of the Horatii* (1785, Louvre). Took an active part in the Revolution, which he further supported with large-scale propaganda pictures. Later became official painter to Napoleon, whom he glorified in several very large canvases still severe in design though warmer in colour. After the Battle of Waterloo, David went to Switzerland, afterwards settling in Brussels, where he died in 1825 (*fig. 86*)

Desportes, Alexandre-François. French painter of still-life and animal compositions, portraits and landscapes, born at Champigneulle in 1661. Worked as a portrait painter in Poland (*c* 1695/6) but soon returned to France, where he won court favour, painting many of the royal dogs for Louis XIV, and providing decorative canvases for many of the royal residences (Anet, Chantilly, etc). In 1712 he paid a visit to England. Died in Paris in 1743 (*fig. 68*)

Drouais, François-Hubert. French portrait painter, born in Paris in 1727. Studied under his father, Hubert Drouais the Elder, and also Boucher. Painted the entire royal family and many of the aristocracy. Patronized by Madame de Pompadour and Madame du Barry. Renowned for his child portraits. Court Painter in 1756,

Drouais exhibited regularly at the Salon 1755–75. Died in Paris in 1775 (*figs. 69 and 70*)

Duplessis, Joseph-Siffrède. French painter, born at Carpentras in 1725. Portrait painter of the second half of the century. Died at Versailles in 1802 (*fig. 71*)

Fragonard, Jean-Honoré. French painter, born at Grasse in 1732. Studied under Chardin and Boucher, whose repertoire of portraits, allegories, mythological paintings and landscapes he took over. Won the Prix de Rome in 1752 and was in Italy 1756–61. Back in France, he was admitted to the Academy in 1765. Died in relative obscurity in Paris in 1806. Fragonard was very versatile and produced portraits, religious and mythological paintings, landscapes and a long series of exquisite drawings in chalk and wash (*figs. 26–34*)

Füssli, Johann Heinrich. Anglo-Swiss painter and draughtsman, born in Zurich in 1741. Studied in Berlin and came to London in 1764. Was at first interested in literature but took to art and 1770–8 lived in Rome, where he greatly admired Michelangelo. Settled again in London in 1778 and died there in 1825. Although many of his attitudes towards style were classically biased, his sense of drama and tension and his vivid imagination, combined with a penchant for romantic illustration, made him a typical figure of the Romantic Movement. An ARA in 1788, RA in 1790, he was Professor of Painting at the Academy 1799–1805, and Keeper from 1804 until his death (*figs. 156–8*)

Gainsborough, Thomas. English landscape and portrait painter, born at Sudbury in Suffolk in 1727. Studied in London 1740–8, and was influenced by Gravelot, Hayman and seventeenth-century Dutch landscapes. 1748–c 1750, worked at Sudbury and then, until 1759, at Ipswich. During these years he painted portraits and landscapes. 1759–74 worked at Bath and emerged as a full-scale portrait

painter. To improve and broaden his style, he studied van Dyck and Rubens, the former influencing his portraits, the latter his landscapes. From 1774 until his death in 1788 lived in London, where he exhibited at the Royal Academy until 1783. Unlike Reynolds and many other portrait painters, he employed very few assistants, preferring to paint in the accessories himself (*figs. 167–9*)

Gillot, Claude. French painter, etcher, theatrical designer and book illustrator, born at Langres in 1673. Came to Paris. Studied under J. B. Corneille and made a reputation with his fantastic arabesque designs; although received into the Academy with a religious subject in 1715. Paved the way for Watteau, who was his pupil, and other eighteenth-century exponents of the genre. Died in Paris in 1722 (*fig. 83*)

Goya y Lucientes, Francisco de. Spanish painter, etcher and lithographer, born at Fuendetodos, near Saragossa, in 1746. Studied with José Luzán at Saragossa in 1760 and in 1766 was in Madrid, where he was a pupil of Francisco Bayeu. After a visit to Italy (1771), he returned to Saragossa but he had settled in Madrid by 1775. 1775–92 he was preoccupied with cartoons for tapestries. Made a court painter in 1786 and First Painter to the King in 1799. Worked for Joseph Bonaparte but regained his royal post with the restoration of Ferdinand VII in 1814. In 1824 settled in France, dying at Bordeaux in 1828 (*figs. 138–51*)

Greuze, Jean-Baptiste. French painter of portraits, allegories and genre scenes, born at Tournus in 1725. Studied under Grandon in Lyons; in Paris was influenced by Dutch genre paintings in private collections. Died in Paris in 1805 (*figs. 63–5*)

Guardi, Francesco. Italian painter of religious and secular subjects and landscapes, born in Venice in 1712. Trained as a figure painter under his brother, Gianantonio Guardi, and collaborated with him on various religious and mythological pictures. Did not adopt view painting as a full time career until after his brother's death in 1760. Died in Venice in 1793 (*figs. 107–18*)

Hogarth, William. English painter and engraver, born in London in 1697. At first apprenticed to a goldsmith but began to engrave at the beginning of the 1720s. Studied at the St Martin's Lane Academy. His first paintings are small-scale conversation pieces but at the beginning of the 1730s he turned to a form of moralizing, satirical illustration, carried out in paintings (e.g. *The Rake's Progress*, 1735) and popularized through engravings. Visited Paris in 1743 and 1748 and was influenced by current French Rococo styles. Died in London in 1764 (*figs. 159–61*)

Hoppner, John. English portrait painter, born in London of German parents in 1758. Entered the Royal Academy Schools in 1775 and first exhibited at the Academy in 1780. Appointed Portrait Painter to the Prince of Wales in 1789, made ARA in 1793 and RA in 1795. Produced very popular portraits, at first influenced by Reynolds and Romney and later by Lawrence, who was his chief rival. Died in London in 1810 (*fig. 174*)

Lancret, Nicolas. French painter of genre scenes and *fêtes-galantes*, born in Paris in 1690. After phase of study with the history painter Pierre Dulin, worked under Gillot. Received into the Académie Royale in 1719 and after the death of Watteau (1721) and Gillot (1722) became very successful with the *fêtes-galantes* and scenes from the Italian Comedy that they had invented. Died in Paris in 1743 (*figs. 35–42*)

Largillière, Nicolas de. French portrait painter, born in Paris in 1656. First trained in Antwerp and later worked in London under Lely, returning to France in 1682. A member of the Academy in 1686 and later its Director. Died in Paris in 1746 (*figs. 59 and 60*)

La Tour, Maurice-Quentin de. French portrait painter, born at Saint-Quentin in 1704. Studied in Paris under J.-J. Spoëde and Dupouch and became a successful exponent of fashionable portraiture. He confined himself to the pastel medium which he handled with great assurance. In 1784 he returned to Saint-Quentin, where he died in 1788 (*fig. 81*)

Lawrence, Sir Thomas, PRA. English portrait painter, born at Bristol in 1769. At first self-taught and something of a child prodigy. Came to London and entered the Royal Academy Schools in 1787. Exhibited at the Academy from 1787 onwards, made ARA in 1791 and RA in 1794. Appointed Painter in Ordinary to the King (George III) in 1792, knighted in 1815 and President of the Royal Academy from 1820 to his death in London in 1830. In every sense the successor to Reynolds, in his day he was unrivalled as a painter of fashionable society and men of action (*figs. 165 and 166*)

Liotard, Jean-Etienne. Swiss painter, mainly of portraits, born in Geneva in 170?. Studied under J. B. Massé in Paris, where he gained a reputation as a fashionable portraitist in oils, pastel, miniature and enamel. Came to specialize in pastel, which he handled with a charm and assurance that brought him European fame. 1738–76 travelled widely, visiting many European courts as well as the Levant, which led him to introduce exotic, Turkish details into some of his work. Also an important collector. Died in Geneva in 1789 (*figs. 154 and 155*)

Longhi, Alessandro. Italian painter and engraver of portraits, born in Venice in 1733. Studied under his father, Pietro Longhi, and also under Giuseppe Nogari. Portrait painter, also engraved the portraits. Died in Venice in 1815 (*fig. 126*)

Longhi, Pietro (known as **Pietro Falca**). Italian genre painter, born in Venice in 1702. Studied under G. M. Crespi at Bologna but in 1734 gave up an unsuccessful career as a history painter in favour of small scenes of contemporary Venetian life. Died in Venice in 1785 (*figs. 122–5*)

Magnasco, Alessandro. Italian painter of fantasy scenes, born in Genoa in 1667. Studied in Milan with Filippo Abbiati, was in Florence *c* 1709–11, but otherwise remained in Milan until 1735, when he settled in his native Genoa, dying there in 1749. Painted a variety of subjects, market scenes, encampments, synagogues and hermits and monks in wild landscapes (*figs. 87 and 88*)

Maulbertsch, Franz Anton. A prolific painter of altarpieces and frescoes in Austria, Hungary, Germany and Bohemia, born at Langenargen on Lake Constance in 1724. Studied in Vienna under Roy. In 1759 made a member of the Viennese Academy, of which he was made a counsellor and professor in 1770. Died in Vienna in 1796 (*fig. 153*)

Meléndez (or Menéndez), Luis Eugenio. Spanish painter of still-life, born in Naples in 1716. Studied under his father and also with Louis-Michel Vanloo; lived in Madrid, where he died in 1780 (*fig. 135*)

Mengs, Anton Raphael. German painter, born in Aussig in Bohemia, in 1728, the son of Ismael Mengs, Court Painter to the Elector of Saxony at Dresden. Went to Rome at an early age and eagerly studied the approved masters, Raphael and the antique, etc. His decisive association with Winckelmann led him to adopt a cold, Neo-Classical style that embodied his friend's theories. Always a declared enemy of the Rococo, Mengs was widely admired in European intellectual circles for his support of the academic tradition. Died in Rome in 1779 (*fig. 137*)

Moreau, Louis-Gabriel, (called Moreau l'Aîné). French landscape painter, born in Paris in 1740. Studied under Demachy, became a member of the Academy of St Luke and Painter to the Comte d'Artois. Worked in oil and gouache and water-colour and produced small views of Paris and its environs. Died in Paris in 1806 (*fig. 85*)

Nattier, Jean-Marc. French portrait painter, born in 1685 in Paris, where he studied under his father, the painter Marc Nattier. In 1715 he went to Amsterdam to paint Peter the Great, the Empress Catherine and members of the Russian Court. Declined an invitation to go to Russia. Died in Paris in 1766 (*fig. 67*)

Oudry, Jean-Baptiste. French painter of history, portraits and animal scenes, born in Paris in 1686. Studied with his father, Jacques Oudry, Michel Serre and Largillière. Became Director of the Beauvais Tapestry Factory in 1733 and Inspector-in-Chief of the Gobelins in 1736. Received into the Academy in 1719 and appointed animal painter to Louis XV. Influenced, in composition and brushwork, by the seventeenth-century Flemish still-life painters. Died at Beauvais in 1755 (*figs. 76 and 77*)

Pannini, Giovanni Paolo. Italian painter, born in Piacenza in 1691 or 1692. Originally an architect, but made his reputation as a landscape painter, specializing in scenes of Roman ruins, sometimes fanciful and sometimes accurate, often mixed, combined with contemporary figures. Also painted straightforward views (e.g. the interior of St Peter's). Influenced Hubert Robert, who made the ruin-motif popular in France. Died in Rome in 1765 (*figs. 127 and 128*)

Paret y Alcázar, Luis. Spanish painter, born at Madrid in 1746. Studied with A. González Velásquez and subsequently with the French painter Charles de la Traverse. 1763–6 and 1767–1771 Paret was in Italy. Strongly influenced by French Rococo styles. He handled a wide range of subject matter: scenes from history, the Bible, mythology, allegory, portraits, genre pieces, landscapes – topographical and otherwise – and still-life. Died in Madrid in 1799 (*fig. 136*)

Pater, Jean-Baptiste. French painter of *fêtes-galantes*, born at Valenciennes, in 1695. Studied with a local master, Jean-Baptiste Guidé. Later moved to Paris, where he came within the orbit of Watteau, who influenced his style in a decisive manner. Next to Lancret the most gifted follower of the master. Received into the Académie Royale in 1728. His oeuvre is large and is characterized by frequent replicas of a favourite design. Died, worn out and over-worked, in Paris in 1736 (*figs. 43–8*)

Perronneau, Jean-Baptiste. French portrait painter, working chiefly in the medium of pastel. Born in Paris in 1715 and trained as an engraver under Laurent Cars. Also studied painting under Natoire and Drouais and in the 1740s was working in close rivalry with the pastellist La Tour. After the mid 1750s he began to travel, visiting Russia, Poland and Holland as well as various French provincial towns. Exhibited at the Salon 1748–79 and became a member of the Académie Royale in 1753. Died in Amsterdam in 1783 (*fig. 75*)

Piazzetta, Giambattista. Italian painter, draughtsman and etcher, born in Venice in 1683. Studied with Antonio Molinari and with G. M. Crespi at Bologna. By 1711 he had returned to Venice, where he settled for life, becoming Director of the Venetian Academy in 1750 and dying in the city in 1754 (*fig. 131*)

Pittoni, Giambattista. Italian painter of religious and mythological subjects, born in Venice in 1687. Studied under his uncle, Francesco Pittoni and later with Antonio Balestra; influenced by Ricci, Piazzetta and G. B. Tiepolo. Elected President of the Venetian Academy of Painting in 1765. Died in Venice in 1767 (*fig. 130*)

Prud'hon, Pierre-Paul. French painter, born in Cluny in 1758. Studied under Devosges at Dijon and went to Paris in 1780. 1784–7 in Italy, where he was influenced by Leonardo and Correg-gio. Executed book illustrations, seals, trophies, and portraits besides large-scale religious and allegorical paintings. Died in Paris in 1823 (*fig. 79*).

Raeburn, Sir Henry, RA. Scottish portrait painter, born at Stockbridge, Edinburgh, in 1756; *c* 1772 apprenticed to a jeweller and began painting miniatures. In 1784 went to London, where he met Reynolds, and in 1785 to Rome. Settled in Edinburgh in 1787 and became a highly successful portrait painter, at first influenced by Reynolds but later developing a broader, more painterly technique. Exhibited regularly at the Royal Academy from 1810, was elected ARA in 1812 and RA in 1815. Knighted in 1822 and appointed King's Limner for Scotland. Died in Edinburgh in 1823 (*figs. 170 and 171*)

Reynolds, Sir Joshua, PRA. English portrait painter and writer on art, and the first President of the Royal Academy, born at Plympton, Devon, in 1723. Studied in London under Hudson (1740–43) and was in Italy 1749–52. Then settled in London, where he died in 1792, and where he became the leading portrait painter of the day with a portrait style that had consciously absorbed many of the lessons of the Grand Manner; Reynolds studied Titian and van Dyck with great intensity. In 1768 elected first President of the Royal Academy, where he exhibited 1769–90, when his sight was impaired and he gave up painting. The celebrated *Discourses*, formal lectures to the students and members of the Academy, were delivered there 1769–90. Painter in Ordinary to George III (*figs. 162–4*)

Ricci, Sebastiano. Italian decorative painter, born at Belluno in 1659. A pupil of Mazzoni and Cervelli and influenced by Veronese and the work of the Baroque decorators that he saw in Rome. Worked in Vienna, London, Paris and various Italian cities, producing mythological and religious works. Elected to the Académie de Peinture in Paris in 1718. Died in Venice in 1734 (*fig. 132*)

Rigaud, Hyacinthe. French portrait painter, born in Perpignan in 1659. Came to Paris in 1681. In 1685 he won the Prix de Rome but did not go to Rome. Became principal portrait painter to the Court of Louis XIV and afterwards worked for Louis XV, evolving for this work a grand style, influenced by van Dyck, in marked contrast to his more intimate and naturalistic portraits of less important sitters. Ran a large and active studio that was kept busy with the flood of orders and the demand for replicas of the royal portraits. Died in 1743 (*figs. 61 and 62*)

Robert, Hubert. French landscape painter, born in Paris in 1733. First studied drawing with the sculptor Slodtz. 1754–65 in Italy, where he was influenced by Pannini, Piranesi and Fragonard, with whom he travelled to Naples in 1761. Made many drawings in red chalk that were to form the basis for the pictures he produced on his return. These were predominantly of classical ruins, either real or imaginary, but he also painted straightforward landscapes. Died in Paris in 1808 (*figs. 55–8*)

Rowlandson, Thomas. English draughtsman and caricaturist, born in London in July of 1756 or 1757. Entered the Royal Academy Schools in 1772 and first exhibited at the Academy in 1775. In the 1780s turned to the genially satirical illustrations of social life on which his reputation depends. He drew the whole of society, from the royal family down to the humblest tavern keeper, in a vivacious style, usually starting with a reed pen and afterwards adding a delicate colour wash. His work was popularized through prints. His later work suffers from haste and over-production. Died in London in 1827 (*fig. 175*)

Tiepolo, Giandomenico. Italian painter, born in Venice in 1727, the son of G. B. Tiepolo, with whom he studied.

Assisted his father at Würzburg (1751–3), at the Villa Valmarana at Vicenza (1757) and in Madrid (1762–70). Later turned to more realistic subjects. Died in 1804 (*figs. 119–21*)

Tiepolo, Giambattista. Italian fresco and easel painter, born in Venice in 1696. Studied under Lazzarini and influenced by Ricci and Piazzetta and the works of Veronese. Travelled widely, working at Udine (1725–8), Milan (1731–40), Bergamo, Würzburg (1752–3), Vicenza (1757), Verona and Strá. In 1755 elected first President of the Venetian Academy. In 1761 invited by Charles III to decorate the Royal Palace at Madrid, where he settled in 1762, dying there in 1770. Employed a great many assistants, who were trained to carry out large-scale fresco work from his small-scale preparatory sketches in oil. A prolific draughtsman. (*figs. 89–98*)

Tocqué, Louis. French portrait painter, born in Paris in 1696. Studied under Bertin and Nattier and became a successful exponent of fashionable, Rococo portraiture. First exhibited at the Salon in 1737; patronized by the Court and also by the bourgeoisie. 1756–8 he worked at the Russian court. Wrote a treatise on portraiture (1750). Died in Paris in 1772 (*fig. 80*)

Troost, Cornelis. Dutch painter of group portraits, genre and theatrical scenes, born in Amsterdam in 1697. The most important eighteenth-century Dutch artist and was much influenced by the work of his seventeenth-century predecessors. Died in Amsterdam in 1750 (*fig. 152*)

Troy, Jean-François de. French decorator and painter of history, genre and portraits, born in Paris in 1679. Trained at the Paris Académie and won a scholarship to study in Italy, where he lived 1699–1706. First painted pseudo-classical compositions but later turned to a more profitable type of genre painting. Produced cartoons for the Gobelins Tapestry Works. Received into the Académie Royale in 1708, becoming professor in 1719. Died in Rome in January, 1752 (*fig. 82*)

Vanloo, Louis-Michel. French painter, mainly of portraits but also of historical subjects, born in Toulon in 1707, the son of Jean-Baptiste Vanloo, with whom he studied. Became an important exponent of the French Rococo style and exhibited at the Paris Salon 1753–69. Worked in Italy and in Spain, where he was made Painter to the King (Philip V), and director of the French Ecole des Elèves Protégés. Died in Paris in 1771 (*fig. 78*)

Vernet, Claude-Joseph. French landscape and sea painter, born at Avignon in 1714, the son of a minor decorative painter, Antoine Vernet, with whom he studied. 1734–53 in Rome, where he was influenced by Claude and Rosa. Became very successful with harbour scenes by sunrise or sunset, stormy seas and landscapes by moonlight that anticipate, to a certain extent, the nineteenth-century Romantic Movement. Made a member of the Roman Academy of St Luke in 1753, a member of the Académie Royale in the same year, in which he was also commissioned to paint a series of the ports of France. Died in Paris in 1789 (*fig. 66*)

Vigée-Lebrun, Elizabeth-Louise. French portrait painter born in Paris in 1755, the daughter of a pastel painter, Louis Vigée, with whom she studied. Also profited from advice given by Doyen, Greuze and Joseph Vernet. Patronized by Marie Antoinette and became a favourite artist of the Court until the Revolution drove her into exile. Worked all over Europe, settled in Switzerland but died in France in 1842 (*fig. 84*).

Watteau, Antoine. French painter, born at Valenciennes in 1684. A pupil in Paris of Claude Gillot and Claude Audran III. Earlier works are mainly military scenes in a style influenced by Teniers but he evolved a poetic genre in which the *fête galante* mingles with elements taken from the Italian Comedy. Also painted portraits and a handful of religious pictures. Received into the Académie Royale in 1717. His technique was not always perfect and some of the paintings have deteriorated. Very influential in his own century. Visited London in 1720. Always suffered from poor health and died at Nogent-sur-Marne in 1721 (*figs. 1–13*)

Wilson, Richard. English landscape painter, born in Penegoes, Wales, in 1714. Went to London in 1729 and was in Italy 1750–7. At first active as a portrait painter but turned to landscape painting in the 1750s. A foundation member of the Royal Academy, whose Librarian he was 1776–82. Died at Llanberis, Wales in 1782 (*fig. 172*)